MENTAL HEALTH MATTERS

UNDERSTANDING BIPOLAR DISORDER

SIMON PIERCE

ROSEN
PUBLISHING

Published in 2026 by The Rosen Publishing Group, Inc.
2544 Clinton Street, Buffalo, NY 14224

Portions of this work were originally authored by Melissa Ambraovitz and Jennifer Mackay and published as *Bipolar Disorder*. All new material this edition authored by Simon Pierce.

Editor: Jennifer Lombardo
Designer: Rachel Rising

Cataloging-in-Publication Data

Names: Pierce, Simon.
Title: Understanding bipolar disorder / Simon Pierce.
Description: First edition. | Buffalo, NY : Rosen Publishing, 2026. | Series: Mental health matters | Includes glossary and index.
Identifiers: ISBN 9781499479669 (pbk.) | ISBN 9781499479676 (library bound) | ISBN 9781499479683 (ebook)
Subjects: LCSH: Bipolar disorder--Juvenile literature.
Classification: LCC RC516.P55 2026 | DDC 616.89'5--dc23

Some of the images in this book illustrate individuals who are models. The depictions do not imply actual situations or events.

Manufactured in the United States of America

CPSIA Compliance Information: Batch #CSRYA26. For further information, contact Rosen Publishing at 1-800-237-9932.

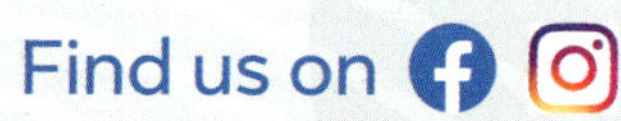

CONTENTS

FOREWORD

There are many misconceptions about illness, especially mental illness. Advances in scientific knowledge have increased our understanding of many diseases and disorders, including the common cold, diabetes, and cancer. Many of these sicknesses and chronic conditions cause physical symptoms that people can see and understand, and their causes are often easy to explain.

The same cannot always be said for mental illnesses. Mental disorders are just as common as physical disorders, but without physical symptoms, they are often dismissed. People tend to believe that a mental illness is easy to get over with enough willpower. They may call people with mental illnesses names such as "lazy" and "attention-seeking." Some people even deny that mental illnesses exist at all.

People who have been convinced by those around them that they have a problem of willpower rather than a treatable illness often go undiagnosed for years. This can cause a lot of suffering; people with an undiagnosed mental disorder often understand that they are experiencing the world in a different way than their peers, but they have no one to turn to for answers. Many feel guilty about not being able to control their symptoms, not realizing that this is as impractical as telling someone with a broken leg that they should be able to walk without pain if they simply try hard enough.

In recent years, the stigma, or perceived shame, of mental illness has decreased. More people, especially young people, are willing to seek therapy and talk openly about their diagnosed mental illnesses. However, this has also led to a rise in misinformation, which can be spread through personal anecdotes, social media, and even news sources. The misuse of "therapy speak" and armchair diagnoses by internet commenters are two growing problems. Furthermore, although the stigma has lessened, it has not disappeared completely. People sometimes use mental illnesses as insults. Someone who displays normal ranges of emotion, for example, may be called "bipolar" as an insult. This shows a lack of understanding about bipolar disorder and furthers the stigma around this disorder by making it sound like a negative aspect of who a person is.

This series aims to offer accurate information about mental illnesses so young adults will have a better understanding of them. Each volume discusses the symptoms of a particular illness, ways it is currently being treated, and the research that is being done to understand it further. Advice for people who may be suffering from a disorder is included, as well as information for their loved ones about how best to support them.

With fully cited quotes, a list of recommended books and websites for further research, and informational charts, this series provides young adults with a factual introduction to common mental illnesses. By learning more about these disorders, they will be better able to show compassion to people who are dealing with mental illnesses and take charge of their own mental health.

ON THE RISE

Since the beginning of the 21st century, the number of diagnosed cases of bipolar disorder (BD) has been on the rise, especially among young people. In the United States, 5.7 million people suffer from BD as of 2018, and doctors suspect that many more remain undiagnosed. BD is a mood disorder characterized by extreme mood and behavior cycles. Someone with BD alternates between periods of mania and depression. Manic episodes include elevated mood, increased energy levels, and often racing or disorganized thoughts, which make it difficult to focus. Depressive episodes include extreme sadness, lack of motivation, increased anxiety, and loss of interest in things the person previously enjoyed. BD can affect anyone of any age, but the National Institute of Mental Health (NIMH) reports that at least half of all cases begin before age 25.

PAST DIAGNOSTIC PROBLEMS

Some experts have proposed that the reason for the increase in diagnoses is that BD used to be underdiagnosed and is currently overdiagnosed. Mental illnesses in general used to be widely underdiagnosed, in part because they carried an even greater stigma, or negative stereotype, than they do today. Being told that a family member had a mental illness was a source of shame for many people, and some people still feel this way, although the stigma has decreased somewhat. This is because in the past, mental illness was generally regarded as a weakness of character rather than what it is: a real disease with biological causes.

In recent years, scientists have proven that diseases such as BD have a biological basis. This has reduced the stigma somewhat, as people are more willing to seek a diagnosis for a condition that is seen as a medical illness than for something that may cause others to label them something offensive, such as "crazy." However, in some communities in the United States and other countries, mental illness still carries a tremendous amount of shame, and people who are part of these communities are often extremely reluctant to admit that they have a mental disorder.

Another factor that led to widespread underdiagnosis of BD in the United States in the recent past was that many patients were misdiagnosed with other disorders. A study reported in 1999 in the *Journal of Affective Disorders* found that doctors did not diagnose BD in 40 percent of the people who should have received this diagnosis. These patients were generally misdiagnosed with major depression, which has all the symptoms of a depressive episode of BD without the manic cycle. For this reason, it is also known as unipolar depression.

Another study found that 50 percent of men who were diagnosed with only drug or alcohol abuse should have also been diagnosed with BD. Other research indicates that 20 to 50 percent of patients diagnosed with schizophrenia, another mental disorder, during the 1970s actually suffered from BD. Misdiagnosis of children is especially common, as several of the hallmarks of BD—especially grandiose sense of self (thinking they are better than everyone else and exaggerating their achievements) and hypersexuality (being unusually preoccupied with sexual fantasies and casual sex)—do not show up until adolescence; this makes some of the symptoms of BD easy to mistake for things such as attention-deficit/hyperactivity disorder (ADHD) in young children.

MISDIAGNOSIS

While BD was underdiagnosed in the past, many experts believe this problem has been overcorrected in the 21st century. The knowledge that BD was underdiagnosed in the past seems to have led some mental health professionals to overdiagnose it in the present day. Complicating matters is the fact that the symptoms of bipolar disorder can be very similar to the symptoms of other mental health issues. For example, impulsivity in spending money is a hallmark of ADHD as well as manic bipolar episodes.

Mental health experts have called for revised diagnostic criteria to reduce the incidence of misdiagnosis. "What the new data on rates of diagnosis suggest is that many children may be misdiagnosed as bipolar because they don't fit neatly into the current diagnostic categories for emotional disorders,"[1] NIMH psychiatrist Ellen Leibenluft told the *New York Times* in 2008.

Other experts believe that the increased awareness of BD among doctors, especially compared to some other mental disorders, has contributed to making it a catchall diagnosis for many mood and behavior disorders. This is primarily a problem with diagnoses from general practitioners and family doctors, who are increasingly responsible for BD diagnoses. Many people do not have the time or money to see a mental health specialist such as a psychiatrist, who may have a waiting list of six months or more and may not be covered under a person's health insurance. This means a doctor such as a general practitioner, who does not have expertise in telling different mental disorders apart, may make an incorrect diagnosis.

Another theory for the increase in BD diagnoses in the United States is that it may have to do with drug companies' influencing of doctors to prescribe expensive new medications. This is a known problem in the medical industry, where some pharmaceutical representatives encourage some doctors to prescribe their medications by bribing them with fancy meals and other expensive gifts. However, although this may be a contributing factor, it is unlikely the only reason for the increase in BD diagnoses. Few studies have been done on BD outside the United States, but one study found that in Denmark, the number of people with BD doubled among both men and women between 1995 and 2012. The researchers concluded that "this increase did not seem to be explained by increased diagnostic attention."[2]

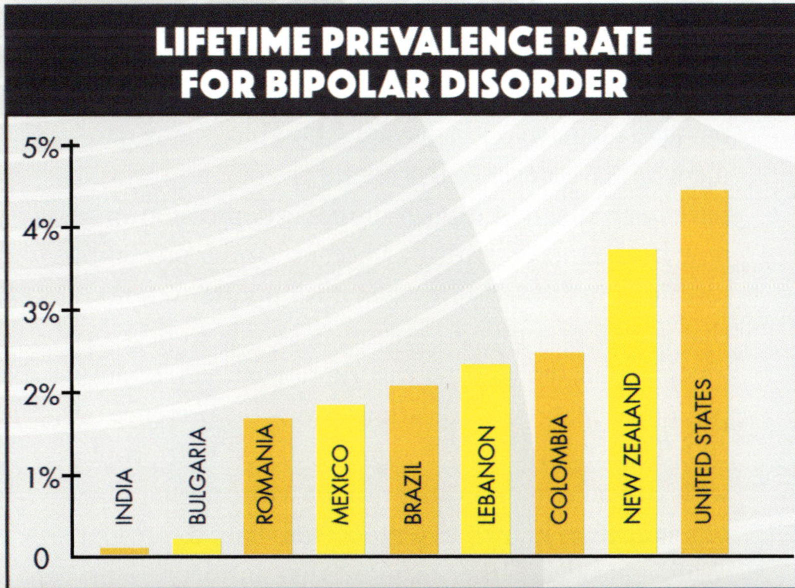

As this information from the American Psychological Association (APA) shows, the United States has a higher rate of BD than many other countries. This may have to do with how informed medical experts in each country are about the symptoms of bipolar disorder and how well they are able to diagnose it.

MORE DIAGNOSES OR MORE CASES?

Another explanation for the increase in BD diagnoses is that more people truly have the disease. No one is sure why this may be true, but several theories have been proposed. Some doctors believe that the increased use of illegal drugs over the past 50 years is to blame. Many studies have shown that substance abuse is one factor that can trigger or worsen a manic or depressive episode. A 2006 study conducted at Mount Sinai Medical School in New York found that about 65 percent of the BD patients seen in the hospital were hospitalized shortly after abusing cocaine, marijuana, hallucinogens, or methamphetamine. However, no one has proven that drug use accounts for the dramatic rise in BD cases, only that it makes the symptoms worse.

Another theory is that a dramatic increase in the use of antidepressant medications is behind the rise in BD. While antidepressants are effective against unipolar depression, they may cause episodes of mania in people who appear to have unipolar depression but actually have undiagnosed BD. Thus, many people who have never had a manic episode and would have been diagnosed with unipolar depression may now be diagnosed with BD because antidepressants revealed the disease. However, it is important to note that antidepressants do not cause people to develop bipolar disorder. If these theories are correct, it simply means that the medications reveal the presence of BD. Some mental health experts suggest that people with BD take their antidepressant with another type of medication known as a mood stabilizer to prevent manic episodes. Others suggest that antidepressants are not good enough at controlling bipolar depression to make it worth the risks associated with them.

Since biological, social, and environmental factors are all believed to play a role in causing BD, some have proposed that a combination of these three factors may underlie the increase in BD diagnoses. These theories, however, have not been scientifically proven.

Better education about mental illness, coupled with increased advocacy, has led to a growing number of people in at-risk populations being aware of BD. This has also led to the reduction of fear and stigma related to seeking treatment for any mental illness. This, in turn, has led to more people being diagnosed with BD because more people are seeking help. Parents are also better able to recognize possible signs in their children because of increased social awareness and are more likely to seek help for their children. Additionally, since recent research has confirmed that BD runs in families, doctors are more likely to consider the possibility that a child has the disorder if a parent or close relative has it as well.

Whatever the true causes for the increasing number of BD cases may be, doctors and advocacy groups believe it is important to take action to understand this trend. BD has a serious impact on individuals, families, and society as a whole, and researchers are currently studying the factors that may be responsible for the rise in cases. Other scientists are attempting to gain a better understanding of the causes of BD in hopes of learning how to prevent, more easily diagnose, and provide better treatments for this increasingly common disease.

CHAPTER ONE

A MISUNDERSTOOD ILLNESS

Medical historians believe BD has affected people throughout history, but no one is known to have related drastic shifts from mania to depression to a single disease until sometime between 30 and 150 CE, when the ancient Greek physician Aretaeus of Cappadocia wrote, "It appears to me that melancholy [depression] is the commencement [beginning] and a part of mania … The development of mania is really a worsening of the disease rather than a change into another disease."[3]

Although Aretaeus made this connection, his idea was not widely acknowledged by the medical community. It was not until 1854 that researchers began considering the possibility that depression and mania could be related. That year, two French doctors independently came to this conclusion and presented papers just two weeks apart. Jules Baillarger coined the term "dual-form insanity" to describe the disorder, while Jean-Pierre Falret called it "circular insanity." Falret was the first to suggest that the disorder had a genetic factor, based on his observation that more than one person in a family often had it.

In 1896, the German psychiatrist Emil Kraepelin was the first to use the term "manic depression"—a term that is still sometimes used today, even though it has fallen out of use within the medical community—in his textbook *Compendium der Psychiatrie*, where he wrote a detailed description of the disease and separated BD from schizophrenia. In the 1980s, psychiatrists who revised the *Diagnostic and Statistical Manual of Mental Disorders (DSM)* changed the official name to "bipolar disorder."

HARD TO DIAGNOSE

One factor that can make bipolar disorder difficult to diagnose is that many patients and those around them do not relate their symptoms to a serious disorder. According to *Psychology Today*:

> *In fact, patients may assume the mania is part of their personality rather than signs of illness. Besides, who can remember "up" episodes when the depressive ones are so low?*
>
> *S. Nassir Ghaemi, director of the Bipolar Disorder Research Program at Emory University, adds that many patients don't have the necessary insight to describe or understand their manic symptoms anyway. In turn, patients don't help the situation by downplaying their symptoms (since bipolar disorder comes with a boatload of stigma). And adding to this confusion is a physician's lack of knowledge about a patient's family history and mood patterns.*[1]

1. Marissa Kristal, "Bipolar Disorder: A Mistaken Diagnosis," *Psychology Today*, last updated June 9, 2016. www.psychologytoday.com/us/articles/200706/bipolar-disorder-mistaken-diagnosis.

MOOD "POLES"

As its name implies, the defining characteristic of BD is extreme shifts between the two "poles" of mania and depression. Doctors use the poles to further classify mood disorders as unipolar (one pole) or bipolar (two poles). People with unipolar disorders experience only one extreme mood state, whereas those with bipolar disorder experience both extremes.

In most cases, the disorder lasts a lifetime once it appears, with episodes of mania alternating with depression. It is thus considered to be a chronic disease. However, the degree and frequency of the mood and behavior shifts in BD vary widely among patients and even within the same person at different times. As the NIMH explained, "Episodes of mania and depression typically come back over time. Between episodes, many people with bipolar disorder are free of changes, but some people may have lingering symptoms."[4]

Bipolar disorder causes intense mood swings, from depression to mania and back again.

Doctors determine the degree of mania or depression on a continuum, or scale, that ranges from normal to severe. The degree of depression is classified as mild, moderate, or severe (also called major) depression. Mania ranges from severe mania down to a condition called hypomania, which has the same symptoms but not the same intensity as true mania. According to Healthline, "Other people will notice if you have hypomania. It causes problems in your life, but not to the extent that mania can."[5] Experts generally distinguish the degree of mania and depression by using standardized questionnaires to assess the impact of these states on an individual's ability to function.

In addition to experiencing varying degrees of manic and depressive episodes, people with BD can also have symptoms of mania and depression at the same time. In the past, doctors called these episodes mixed states, but now they are officially known as a manic, hypomanic, or depressive episode with mixed features. This is what medical professionals call a specifier—a term that can add more detail to an official diagnosis. Some people who are unfamiliar with the new terminology may still call them mixed states.

MANIA SYMPTOMS

Patients in a manic state often report feeling energetic, "high," happy, outgoing, jumpy, irritable, invincible, and very creative. One woman described her mania like this: "I feel like I have a motor attached. Everything is moving slowly, and I want to go, go, go. I feel like one of those toys that somebody winds up and sends spinning or doing cartwheels or whatever."[6]

During a manic episode, people often behave recklessly. They may drive too fast, spend too much money, or quit their job without having a plan for the future.

Manic people may talk fast, have racing thoughts, and jump from one project or idea to another without finishing any of them. They sleep little and often launch ambitious projects because they believe they can accomplish anything they try. While manic, some people with BD do impulsive and risky things, such as quitting a job, spending a lot of money, having unprotected sex with multiple partners, or engaging in other risk-taking activities that can be dangerous; this behavior is due to a feeling of being invincible—the belief that nothing bad can happen to them, sometimes also referred to as grandiosity—that some BD patients experience while manic. Some may be angry and violent toward others or themselves. People in a manic or hypomanic state are often unlikely to seek medical help because mania generally creates positive feelings. Instead of feeling like there is a problem, therefore, patients often feel very good and mistake those good feelings for the typical good moods that everyone experiences sometimes.

DEPRESSION SYMPTOMS

People in a depressed state, on the other hand, are more likely to seek help because they feel overwhelmingly sad, helpless, and hopeless. The individual's energy and grandiose plans evaporate, and extreme tiredness sets in, making it difficult for them to perform normal tasks such as cooking, cleaning, or going to work. The person may either have trouble sleeping or may sleep most of the time. Many depressed people do not feel like getting out of bed at all; they lose interest in activities they once enjoyed and often isolate themselves from their friends and family. Concentrating and making decisions becomes overwhelming. The person may eat too much or not enough and will frequently have unexplained aches and pains. Some depressed people attempt suicide.

MIXED FEATURES

People with episodes that have mixed features experience elements of both mania and depression. They are often agitated and energetic, but also feel sad and hopeless. The term "with mixed features" is generally added to the state the person has been in most recently. For instance, for someone who had been in a manic episode for a week and still feels symptoms of mania but also starts to feel some symptoms of depression, their mood would be described as a manic episode with mixed features.

Those with mixed feature episodes, just as with mania or depression, may abuse drugs and alcohol, which can worsen other symptoms of the disease. BD has the highest rate of dual diagnosis with substance abuse of any mental illness. There are many theories for why this is. One is that people with BD self-medicate with drugs and alcohol in an attempt to give themselves relief from their intense emotions. This is especially true if they are unable or unwilling to see a psychiatrist who can prescribe medication, or if their prescribed medication is not working. Another is that, since people with uncontrolled BD often have poor impulse control, they may find it difficult to stop themselves from drinking too much or doing drugs when these substances are available.

In a depressive episode, a person may feel hopeless, worthless, and have little to no energy.

However, there is no answer that is completely true for everyone with BD, and scientists are still doing research into this issue. Those with a dual diagnosis of BD and substance abuse face unique challenges in treatment.

Those in manic or depressive states, with or without mixed features, may also have psychotic symptoms, such as delusions and hallucinations. A delusion is a false belief, such as the idea that someone is trying to hurt them. There is no visible evidence for a delusion. Hallucinations are false sensory perceptions, such as hearing voices or seeing things. Delusions and hallucinations contribute to the inability to distinguish fantasy from reality that characterizes psychosis. The delusions an individual has seem to depend on whether they are manic or depressed. Thus, someone who is manic and psychotic may falsely believe they are famous, are wealthy, or have superpowers. A depressed psychotic patient may think they are a failure or a criminal, regardless of the truth.

Although the specific symptoms of BD vary among individuals, the general characteristics of the disease are consistent and have remained consistent over time. Descriptions of symptoms by doctors today are remarkably similar to those by doctors throughout history. Aretaeus, for example, wrote:

> *They with whose madness joy is associated, laugh, play, dance night and day, and sometimes go openly to the market crowned, as if victors in some contest of skill ... Others have madness attended with anger; and these sometimes rend [rip] their clothes and kill their keepers, and lay violent hands upon themselves ... They are also given to extraordinary phantasies [fantasies] ... They are of a changeable temper, their senses are acute, they are suspicious, irritable without any cause, and unreasonably desponding [hopeless] when the disease tends to gloom.*[7]

KIDS AND TEENS

The greatest differences in symptoms become apparent when comparing children and adolescents with BD to adults suffering from BD. According to the *Medifocus Guidebook on Bipolar Disorder*:

> *Onset of bipolar disorder during childhood and adolescence appears to be a more severe form of bipolar than adult onset and there tends to be more psychosis involved ... Children and adolescents also tend*

EXAMPLES OF PSYCHOSIS

Psychosis is a detachment from reality that makes people unable to recognize what is actually happening around them. It can be very frightening, both for the person experiencing it and the people around them. Andrea Paquette, the founder and executive director of a Canadian nonprofit organization called the Stigma-Free Society, described some of the experiences she had during psychosis that was triggered by a manic episode:

> *I drafted a thirty-three page Canadian Federal election strategy that I believed would win the next election. I naturally poised myself as the next Prime Minister of Canada … I soon began to have one-on-one conversations with God, but during this time, I could actually hear his responses in my own mind … I actually witnessed [in a hallucination] fire missiles being thrown at me, but they beamed off my body as if I were wearing an invisible shield. I soon believed that I was Eve from the Garden of Eden. It was amazing because I thought that I had finally figured out who I was, and how was it possible that I had not known all these years?*[1]

1. Andrea Paquette, "My Bipolar Psychotic Break—Myth or Meaningful,?" *bp*, April 19, 2015. www.bphope.com/blog/my-bipolar-psychotic-break-myth-or-meaningful.

> *to experience very rapid mood swings many times a day. It is common to see children experience depressive states in the morning that is followed by increasing energy and mania later in the afternoon or evening.*[8]

Adults, too, can experience rapidly shifting moods, known as rapid cycling, but rarely do these shifts occur daily as is often seen in children and teens.

Young people with BD also tend not to have periods of recovery in between episodes. They may go for months or years with continuous illness. The behaviors seen in young people with BD are also more likely to include explosive temper tantrums and aggression, as well as long stretches of crying. Afterward, the child may suddenly start laughing hysterically for no reason, which may last for only a while, followed by another episode of explosive anger.

Some of the extreme behaviors seen in children with BD are not out of the ordinary for their age. For example, many kids test their limits to see if they have superpowers, especially after first discovering superhero movies and comic books.

It is normal for children to have trouble regulating their emotions, but a child with bipolar disorder will generally show more intense mood swings than others their age.

A child with BD might continue to believe they have powers even if they never do anything extraordinary, while a child without the disorder will soon realize they cannot fly, turn invisible, or perform other supernatural feats and will give up on the idea.

Other behaviors are inappropriate for the person's age. For example, BD commonly has sexual symptoms, including risky sexual behaviors, such as having casual sex frequently with multiple different partners. This can be dangerous to a person's health at any age. Someone who is in a manic state and believes they are invincible will be less likely to bother with protective measures such as condoms, which means a higher risk of sexually transmitted diseases (STDs) and pregnancy. According to Everyday Health, if risky sexual behaviors are "combined with other risky behaviors like smoking, heavy drinking, substance abuse, not getting enough sleep, and poor diet, it can contribute to several chronic diseases."[9] High-risk sex can also have a negative effect on a person's emotional health. Someone who engages in it while they are in a manic episode may feel bad about their actions when they cycle to a depressive episode. Although these behaviors are more often seen in adults, sometimes children with BD—even very young ones—are sexually active.

Not all children with BD have constant, intense symptoms; in some cases, mild depression or hypomania gradually worsen over time and go on to develop into full-blown bipolar disorder later on. In other instances, a child may have some symptoms of BD, but no one suspects that anything is wrong. Family members may simply label the child as "moody" or "socially withdrawn," or as being "very energetic" or a "daredevil." As with adults, the boundaries between normal ups and downs and BD may be difficult to distinguish. If professional help is sought, it may take awhile to get an accurate diagnosis.

DIAGNOSTIC CONFUSION

The fact that BD can be mistaken for other disorders is one factor that can make diagnosis in people of any age difficult. According to a 2016 study, the average time from the onset of symptoms to a proper diagnosis is six years. According to study leader Matthew Large, a professor of psychiatry at the University of New South Wales in Australia, "While some patients, particularly those who present with psychosis, probably do receive timely treatment, the diagnosis of the early phase of bipolar disorder can be difficult … The diagnosis of bipolar disorder can also be missed because it relies on a detailed life history and corroborative information from careers and family, information that takes time and care to gather."[10] For adults, BD is most often misdiagnosed as unipolar depression, while for young people, it is frequently dismissed completely as normal teenage moodiness.

One of the illnesses that is most commonly misdiagnosed as BD (or vice versa) in children is ADHD, which is characterized by hyperactivity,

A NEW CATEGORY

Diagnosis of mental disorders, including BD, are based on criteria set forth in the *Diagnostic and Statistical Manual of Mental Disorders, 5th Edition (DSM-5)*. This edition came out in 2013, so people who were diagnosed years ago using the previous edition, *DSM-IV*, may use terms to describe themselves that have been changed or deleted from the newest edition.

According to the website Verywell:

> *Even though childhood bipolar disorder has been well-defined and used (though not listed in the DSM-IV) for many years, pediatric bipolar disorder is not a new diagnosis in the DSM-5. Instead, children with such symptoms will most likely fall into either the category of Disruptive, Impulse Control, and Conduct Disorders, or into a diagnosis that is part of the category of Depressive Disorders, called Disruptive Mood Dysregulation Disorder.*[1]

Disruptive mood dysregulation disorder (DMDD) is a new diagnosis, classified for the first time in the *DSM-5*. NIMH summarized it:

> *DMDD symptoms typically begin before the age of 10, but the diagnosis is not given to children under 6 or adolescents over 18. A child with DMDD experiences:*
>
> - *Irritable or angry mood most of the day, nearly every day*
> - *Severe temper outbursts (verbal or behavioral) at an average of three or more times per week that are out of keeping with the situation and the child's developmental level*
> - *Trouble functioning due to irritability in more than one place (e.g., home, school, with peers)*
>
> *To be diagnosed with DMDD, a child must have these symptoms steadily for 12 or more months.*[2]

1. Marcia Purse, "What Is the DSM-5,?" Verywell, last updated April 20, 2018. www.verywellmind.com/what-is-the-dsm-5-379955.

2. "Disruptive Mood Dysregulation Disorder," National Institute of Mental Health, last updated January 2017. www.nimh.nih.gov/health/topics/disruptive-mood-dysregulation-disorder-dmdd/disruptive-mood-dysregulation-disorder.shtml.

distractibility, an inability to concentrate, and sometimes rapid talking. Doctors must ask a lot of questions about the child's behavior to find small clues that help with a diagnosis. For instance, a child with ADHD who is too energetic to sleep much will often be tired the next morning, while a child with BD will generally continue being energetic. Doctors distinguish BD from ADHD primarily by the fact that unlike ADHD, BD includes grandiose delusions, hypersexuality, elation, and a decreased need for sleep. ADHD also does not include alternating episodes of mania and depression.

The Child Mind Institute noted, "The low frustration tolerance of ADHD does not go away, while a child with bipolar disorder could be severely irritable for six months and then not have another episode for years."[11] Sometimes, however, the symptoms of BD and ADHD are so similar that misdiagnosis occurs. The fact that many children and adolescents with BD also have ADHD further complicates diagnosis. In such cases, making a dual diagnosis can be especially challenging.

The fact that BD often occurs with several other disorders besides ADHD adds to the complexity of diagnosis. The most common is substance abuse; between 40 and 60 percent of people with BD also

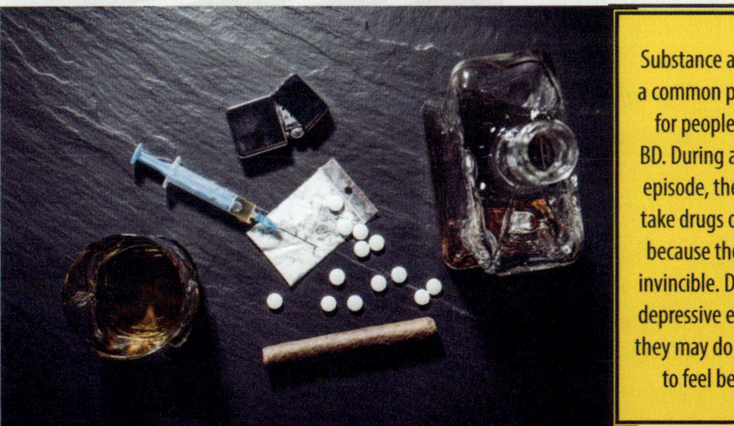

Substance abuse is a common problem for people with BD. During a manic episode, they may take drugs or drink because they feel invincible. During a depressive episode, they may do it to try to feel better.

have a substance use disorder at some point in their lifetime. Other commonly co-occurring disorders are post-traumatic stress disorder (PTSD)—which can develop after a traumatic event, such as being sexually assaulted—and anxiety disorders.

Other disorders that are often confused with BD are antisocial personality disorder, conduct disorder, and borderline personality disorder (BPD). BPD shares some qualities with BD but is not episodic. Typically, people with BPD are continuously impulsive, angry, and irritable, and sometimes its symptoms resemble those in rapid cycling BD, so it may be difficult for a doctor to distinguish which disorder a patient has.

Major depression and schizophrenia are also often misdiagnosed as BD, and vice versa. Generally, if these disorders are observed by a professional over time, the distinctions between them and BD become clearer. Most types of schizophrenia are characterized by delusions and hallucinations more than by extreme emotional moods. However, one disorder, called schizoaffective disorder, which is closely related to schizophrenia, shares symptoms with both schizophrenia and BD, and it is often very difficult for a doctor to distinguish it from BD.

With major depression, misdiagnosis most often occurs when a patient with BD sees a doctor only during depressive episodes. Andy Behrman, author of *Electroboy: A Memory of Mania*, had this experience:

> *For more than ten years, I was consistently misdiagnosed with depression by more than eight mental health care professionals … In a nutshell, I was being diagnosed improperly because I only visited these doctors during my "low points" or depression; I was not accurately filling them in on my symptoms, and they were not asking enough questions about my mental illness. In retrospect, had I shared more information with them perhaps it*

would have been easier for them to diagnose me with bipolar disorder.[12]

LOOKING FOR CLUES

Difficulties in making an accurate diagnosis is one factor that contributes to the often lengthy diagnostic process that begins when a person seeks help from a medical professional. The doctor will conduct a physical examination, order laboratory tests, take a medical history, and have the patient complete a standardized mental evaluation and questionnaires to help with diagnosis. There are no obvious physical or biochemical signs of bipolar disorder, but a physical exam, blood tests, and imaging tests can help the doctor rule out other medical problems, such as a brain tumor, that might be contributing to the patient's symptoms. The medical history will tell the doctor about the person's family history of mental illness, which can play a role in increasing the likelihood of BD, and about the individual's previous medical problems. If a doctor is reasonably sure that the patient has a mental disorder such as BD, they will generally make a referral to a psychiatrist, which is a medical doctor who specializes in mental illnesses.

A psychiatrist can help a patient with BD determine the right type and dose of medication to control their symptoms. Sometimes this takes a little trial and error.

The doctor bases a diagnosis of BD on criteria set forth in the *Diagnostic and Statistical Manual of Mental Disorders (DSM)*. The book is now in its fifth edition (*DSM-5*), and it specifies several basic types of the disease that are slightly different than the criteria in previous editions. The first type, bipolar I disorder, is the most severe and typical form. Patients have severe manic and depressive episodes that differ significantly from previous behavior. Manic episodes must last at least seven days (less if hospitalization is required to prevent the patient from harming themselves or others), and depressive episodes must last at least two weeks. Symptoms must include at least three in a list of characteristic behaviors and must be severe enough to cause noticeable difficulties at home, school, or work.

Bipolar II disorder is less severe than bipolar I and is characterized by depressive episodes alternating with hypomania, but not full-blown mania. The *DSM-IV* specified that people who had experienced episodes with mixed features could not be diagnosed with bipolar II, but this exclusion was removed in the *DSM-5*. People with either bipolar I or II may also be diagnosed with rapid cycling; this involves having four or more episodes of major depression, mania, or hypomania—with or without mixed features—within one year. In contrast, people with untreated BD who do not have rapid cycling generally have manic episodes that last about three to six months and depressive episodes that last about six months to a year.

The third type, cyclothymic disorder, or cyclothymia, is the mildest form of BD. It includes episodes of hypomania that alternate with mild depression for at least two years for adults and one year for children and adolescents. Criteria for hypomania include three or more of the symptoms of mania that last at least four days but do not require hospitalization; do not lead to significant difficulties at school, at work, or in social relationships; and do not involve psychosis. The criteria for other types of BD are not met with this diagnosis.

Three other types of BD exist in the *DSM-5*: substance-induced bipolar disorder, bipolar disorder associated with another medical condition, and bipolar disorder not elsewhere classified. Substance-induced BD, as the name implies, is caused by a drug. However, it does not have to be an illegal or recreational drug such as cocaine or alcohol. Some prescribed drugs react with an individual's body chemistry to give them depression or mood swings. In the case of recreational drugs, which people often use to self-medicate in the hope that the drugs will make them feel better, it can be difficult for someone to realize that the drugs are actually making their symptoms worse. It can also be difficult for someone to tell what is happening when the drug they are taking is not meant to treat their mood. For instance, some antibiotics are known to cause depression, but a person may not connect their antibiotic with their changed mood. When the true cause is identified and use of the drug is discontinued, the symptoms generally clear up.

Bipolar disorder associated with another medical condition, like substance-induced BD, has an outside cause. For instance, someone who has had a stroke—an interruption in the brain's blood supply that can kill someone or cause damage to parts of the brain—may have changes in their mood after they recover from their stroke. Bipolar disorder not elsewhere classified—also called bipolar disorder not otherwise specified, or bipolar NOS—is used when a person meets most but not all of the criteria for one of the other types of BD. For instance, the

CRITERIA OF MANIA AND DEPRESSION

Criteria for a manic episode include three or more of the following that last for at least one week (less if hospitalization is necessary):

- inflated self-esteem, where the person believes they are better than others or are capable of doing things more quickly than is reasonable (for instance, writing a 10-page paper in half an hour)
- needing little sleep
- talking quickly and feeling unable to stop speaking, even when others try to speak
- racing thoughts that are repetitive, are fragmented, or make little sense
- being easily distracted or overly fixated (either leaving tasks undone or working on them without rest for hours or days at a time)
- physical agitation such as pacing or fidgeting
- increased goal-directed activity that is not sustained after the manic episode ends; for instance, planning to open a business but never following through
- inappropriate behavior that does not seem inappropriate to the person with BD
- engaging in risky activities, such as hypersexual behaviors, spending sprees, foolish business investments, or driving too fast

Criteria for a major depressive episode include five or more of the following over two weeks:

- depressed mood most of the day, nearly every day, including tearfulness, sadness, or irritability
- loss of interest in activities the person normally enjoys
- significant weight loss or weight gain and increase or decrease in appetite
- inability to sleep or sleeping too much
- slowed behavior
- fatigue and loss of energy
- feelings of worthlessness or unreasonable guilt
- inability to concentrate and make decisions
- recurrent thoughts of death or suicide, or attempted suicide

person may have alternating manic and depressive episodes, but they may not last long enough to meet the criteria for bipolar I or II. Bipolar NOS may seem like a diagnosis that is not specific enough to be helpful, but it is actually important because it allows people to get help and treatment even when their mental illness does not fit neatly into one specific category.

Whatever type of bipolar disorder a person has, it generally worsens over time without treatment. For this reason, doctors emphasize that getting an accurate diagnosis as soon as possible is important for helping to prevent increased frequency and severity of episodes. Many patients, though, wait years before seeking help, and the consequences can be devastating. As one man wrote, "I've always had mood swings. I used to throw huge tantrums when I was a kid. As I got older, the highs got higher and the lows got lower. I lost several jobs and ruined a whole bunch of relationships. Finally, I decided nothing could be worse than living like I was, and I went to get some help."[13]

MULTIPLE CAUSES

The symptoms and diagnosis of BD are not the only things about the disorder that are complex. The causes, too, are complicated and involve diverse interactions among many factors. For many years, the medical community has held varied—and often incorrect—ideas about what these causes are. For instance, the ancient Greek physician Aretaeus believed the disorder resulted from "want of purgation of the system,"[14] which meant the body could not get rid of waste materials. This accumulation of waste in the body, Aretaeus wrote, led to problems with the brain. During the Middle Ages, most people—even doctors—thought demons or witches caused mental illnesses. In the 1600s, some experts began to see that although the ancient Greeks had not identified the true cause of mental illnesses, their idea that physical abnormalities could contribute to mental illnesses was more accurate than the theory that supernatural forces were to blame for people's behavioral and mood changes.

Although great advances in medicine and technology have been made since the 1600s, doctors today are still unsure of the exact causes of BD. According to Medical News Today, "Bipolar disorder does not appear to have a single cause but is more likely to result from a range of factors that interact."[15] Research has proven that genes do play a

COMPUTER IMAGING

Modern technology allows doctors to study the structure and activity of the brain. This helps them determine which abnormalities underlie diseases such as bipolar disorder. Frequently used technologies include the following:

- Computerized tomography/computerized axial tomography (CT/CAT) uses X-rays to create cross-sectional computer-generated pictures of the brain. CT/CAT provides much more detail than conventional X-rays do.
- Magnetic resonance imaging (MRI) uses radio waves and magnetic fields to generate computer images of structures in the brain. It uses no radiation and provides more detailed images of soft tissue than CT does but is more expensive.
- Functional magnetic resonance imaging (fMRI) is similar to MRI but uses technology that, instead of structure, measures blood flow to monitor which areas of the brain are active during certain activities.
- Magnetic resonance spectroscopy (MRS) uses magnetic fields to measure brain chemicals and is useful in assessing and diagnosing the biochemical causes of some diseases.
- Positron emission tomography (PET) uses radioactive tracers injected into the bloodstream to measure brain structure and function, such as blood flow, oxygen use, and metabolism. The PET scanner detects and records the energy given off by the tracer, and a computer converts this information into three-dimensional pictures. Unlike MRI and CT, PET can detect tiny cellular changes.

role, but how much of a role is still debatable. Other possible causes include imbalances in brain chemicals such as neurotransmitters and hormones, as well as a traumatic event that can potentially trigger BD symptoms.

NO SINGLE CAUSE

Through research conducted over the past few decades, experts now know that BD results from complex interactions between biological, social, and environmental factors rather than having a single cause.

No one is certain about precisely which combinations of biological, social, and environmental factors cause BD, but experts do know that having a parent or sibling with the disease, having a great deal of stress or trauma in one's life, abusing drugs and alcohol, and certain differences in brain structure are some of the main risk factors that increase an individual's likelihood of developing the illness.

The finding that having a family history of BD significantly raises the risk of getting the disease has led scientists to conclude that genes play a causal role. Genes are made up of deoxyribonucleic acid (DNA) and pass hereditary information from parents to their offspring. Genetic information is found in thread-like bodies called chromosomes in the nucleus of each body cell. The sequence of chemicals that compose genes encodes a set of instructions telling the cell how to operate and produce essential proteins.

Genetic information and gene mutations, or abnormalities, can be inherited directly or inherited as a predisposition. Examples of genetic traits that are passed on directly include hair color and eye color. Individuals who inherit the genes or mutations for these qualities show certain characteristics or develop certain diseases regardless of environmental events.

In contrast, a genetic predisposition means someone has the genes or mutations that are responsible for the characteristic or disease, but they might never

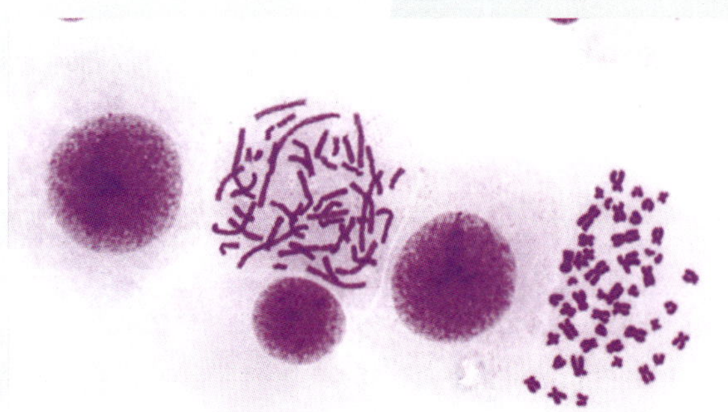

Genes play a large role in determining whether or not someone will develop a physical or mental illness. However, this process is more complex than most people realize.

know it. In many cases, the inherited traits will not become apparent unless triggering environmental events are also present. Scientists believe a genetic predisposition is involved in causing bipolar disorder.

BIPOLAR DISORDER IN FAMILIES

One piece of evidence that led scientists to conclude that a genetic predisposition plays a role in causing BD is that the disease tends to run in families. Children who have a biological parent or sibling with BD are four to six times more likely than other children to develop the disorder. When both parents have BD, that risk increases even more. However, risk is not the same as a guarantee; many people with a family history of BD never develop the disorder themselves. Other aspects of the disease, such as the age at which a person's first manic episode occurs and the number and frequency of episodes, are also often consistent within families, according to scientific research.

Identical twins have basically identical genes, but this does not guarantee that they will have the same disorders. This shows that genes are not the only factor that determines whether someone will develop bipolar disorder.

Studies of identical twins, who share basically identical genes, have also proven a genetic link. When one twin has BD, the other twin also has it 40 to 70 percent of the time. Nonidentical, or fraternal, twins, who share only about 50 percent of their genes, both have BD less than 10 percent of the time. "That tells us that about two-thirds of the risk for bipolar disorder can be explained by genes,"[16] said Dr. Francis J. McMahan of NIMH. Other researchers place their estimates even higher, saying genetics account for as much as 85 percent of the risk.

Scientists have also determined that several gene mutations are linked to BD. Not all people with the disease have each mutation. Researchers identify genes linked to a particular disorder by studying the genome (the complete DNA signature) of people with and without the disorder. In 2021, researchers published the results of the largest genetic study of bipolar disorder to ever be performed. They found 64 different parts of the genome that had an effect on bipolar disorder—more than twice as many as they had previously known about.

Through previous studies, researchers had already linked BD to abnormalities in several genes that control the production and regulation of neurotransmitters such as serotonin, norepinephrine, dopamine, and glutamate. These chemicals all contribute to mood, energy levels, and thought processes. One such gene is the human serotonin transporter gene, which is important in regulating mood and sleep. Defects in genes that regulate calcium and sodium channels, or gates, on the surface of nerve cells have also been shown to play a role in BD. The *CACNA1C* gene, for example, determines whether or not a nerve cell, or neuron, will let certain brain chemicals flow in or out. This, in turn, determines whether or not the neuron will fire and pass along messages to other neurons. Researchers have linked the abnormal nerve firing that results from defective *CACNA1C* genes to the development of BD.

Other mutations linked to BD affect some of the genes that control a person's circadian rhythms, or internal biological clock. For this reason, they are often called "clock genes." They control the release of chemicals that, when functioning normally, make people feel awake and alert during the day and sleepy at night. People with these mutations are especially likely to experience relapses, or recurrences, of episodes after periods of inadequate sleep. Some researchers believe that people with BD "may have a molecular clock that is unable to properly adapt to changes in the environment,"[17] according to psychiatrist C. A. McClung of the University of Texas Southwestern Medical Center. One 2012 study found that variations in about half of the known clock genes were linked to BD. Further evidence that disruptions in biological rhythms are involved in BD comes from studies showing that people with the disease are likely to have more depressive episodes in winter, when it is darker, and more manic episodes in summer, when it is light more often. The biological clock is influenced by seasonal variations in daylight.

However, other researchers believe the pattern is the other way around—BD disrupts circadian rhythms. A 2018 study conducted in the United Kingdom (UK) found that disruptions in the sleep-wake cycle are strongly related to BD and other mood disorders, but the researchers could not say for certain which one was the original cause because it was a study that observed behavioral patterns rather than genetics and body chemistry. More research will need to be done to determine what is known as the direction of causality.

Discoveries of other mutations linked to BD, as well as to other mental disorders, indicate that genes that govern the development of psychotic symptoms and the brain's response to some drugs play a role in determining a genetic predisposition to multiple mental illnesses. For example, a 2018 study that was published in the journal *Science* found "patterns of genetic activity that overlap with five major psychiatric disorders: alcoholism, autism, bipolar disorder, depression, and schizophrenia."[18] Identifying

GENES AND TREATMENT

In 2022, researchers found that one specific gene, called *AKAP11*, has a larger-than-average effect on bipolar disorder than most other genes. It is not solely responsible for causing the disorder, but it appears to be more directly linked than some other genes.

Identifying *AKAP11* has already led researchers to start planning other studies. They want to learn things such as exactly how the gene variations affect people and what kind of treatments can work well with it. For example, a medication called lithium has been used for many years to treat the effects of bipolar disorder. Doctors have known for some time that lithium does not work well for everyone, although it was unclear exactly why this was.This lack of clarity made it hard for them to find better treatments because they could not solve a problem they did not understand. Now, researchers say *AKAP11* interacts with a pathway in the brain that is clearly affected by lithium. There is a possibility that in the future, after more studies are done, health-care professionals will be able to tell who will respond well to lithium, why the drug works, and what they can use in its place for people who do not respond well.

similarities in the brains of people with mental disorders could make it easier for doctors to diagnose and treat people in the future. Currently, relying on people to accurately describe the type and frequency of their symptoms makes the diagnosis and treatment process difficult, so having a visible symptom would increase doctors' accuracy.

LOOKING AT THE BRAIN

The genetic mutations that underlie BD in turn result in abnormal brain activity and structure that directly contribute to causing the disorder. Brain imaging techniques such as magnetic resonance imaging (MRI), functional magnetic resonance imaging (fMRI), magnetic resonance spectroscopy (MRS), and positron emission tomography (PET) allow doctors to take pictures and study brain chemicals and activity inside the brain. Many studies have shown that the brains of people with BD differ both from those of healthy people and from those with certain other mental disorders. According to the authors of *Living with Someone Who's Living with Bipolar Disorder*, "Unlike many brain disorders such as a tumor or stroke, BD is not localized to one part of the brain. It involves abnormalities of several regions of diffuse [scattered] functions."[19]

Structural abnormalities in the brains of BD patients include thinning of the brain's gray matter, causing decreased size and cell density in parts of the brain that are involved in regulating thoughts and emotions. These parts show abnormal activity as well as structural abnormalities. For instance, scientists have linked lowered brain activity and abnormal firing between neurons in the right prefrontal cortex with symptoms of mania.

Another brain area, called the amygdala, also appears to play a role in causing BD. As psychiatrist Ellen Leibenluft of the NIMH explained, "The amygdala tells us what in our environment is emotionally important. It seems to be acting differently in bipolar disorder, in both adults and children. We see an increased activity in the amygdala in response to emotional triggers in the environment."[20]

The amygdala communicates with the prefrontal cortex to analyze emotional responses. When the prefrontal cortex is not working enough due to thinning gray matter and the amygdala is working too much, it creates an inappropriate emotional response to situations and stimuli, which may be the basis of the manic and depressive symptoms experienced by people with BD.

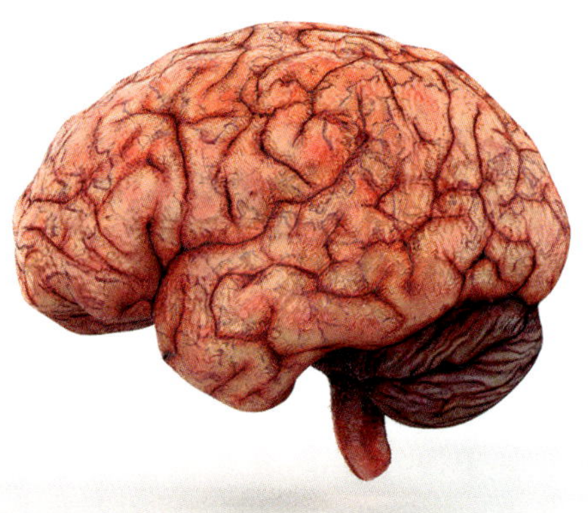

The structure and function of a person's brain plays a large role in whether they have bipolar disorder and what symptoms they exhibit. Because everyone's brain is different, this creates challenges for doctors who are trying to find the right treatment for their patients.

Other research indicates that some of the abnormal brain activity seen in people with BD may result from altered synapses and nerve cell plasticity, or the ability of neural circuits to change. Synapses are tiny gaps between neurons. Neurons communicate with each other by sending chemical and electrical signals across these synapses. Signals are sent by long nerve cell extensions called axons and received by receptors on shorter branches called dendrites.

Several researchers cite evidence that some gene mutations associated with BD produce abnormal activity in synapses. This, in turn, is associated with defects in nerve plasticity, which is essential for normal brain operations. Plasticity allows the brain to adapt to internal and external conditions. One cell part that regulates plasticity is the mitochondrion, or cell powerhouse. Studies have shown that defects in cell energy production lead to altered synapses and plasticity. This makes many scientists believe that BD results at least partly from an inability of brain cells and circuits to communicate and adapt to changing conditions. Researchers are currently attempting to gain a better understanding of how these processes work in hopes of further untangling the complex biological causes of BD.

ESTROGEN AND TESTOSTERONE

Many experts believe that sex hormones also play a role in causing the brain changes that underlie BD. They have reached this conclusion because most cases of the disease begin during adolescence and young adulthood, when sex hormones become active. The relationship between sex hormones and BD, however, is not yet clear. Scientists do know that sex hormones affect the brain in various ways and that people who are assigned male at birth (AMABs) and people who are assigned female at birth (AFABs) experience BD at about equal rates, but with some different symptoms. Estrogen, the primary female hormone, enhances the activity of the neurotransmitters serotonin, norepinephrine, dopamine, and gamma-aminobutyric acid (GABA) in the brain. All of these neurotransmitters regulate emotion. AFABs with BD are more likely to experience depressive episodes than manic episodes, and some experts believe it is because of the way estrogen interacts with these neurotransmitters.

Some experts say hormone imbalances are often mistaken for BD, leading to overdiagnosis of the disorder. Others disagree, citing research that has been done on brain structure. For example, a study from the University of California at its Berkeley and Davis campuses showed that after menopause (the time when a menstruating person stops getting a period), someone who does not take estrogen supplements has less activity in several areas of the cerebral cortex and smaller volume in the hippocampus compared with those who take these supplements.

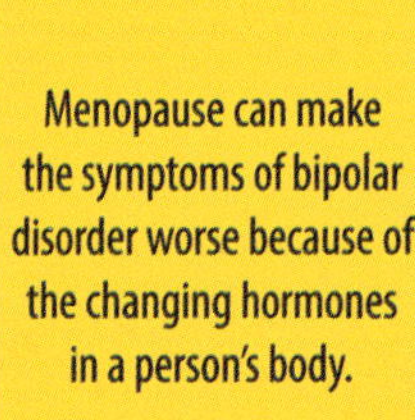

Menopause can make the symptoms of bipolar disorder worse because of the changing hormones in a person's body.

Lower levels of progesterone, which is another female sex hormone, have also been associated with bipolar disorder. It is unclear whether these low levels cause BD symptoms or whether the disorder lowers progesterone levels, but some experts suggest that taking progesterone supplements can help stabilize symptoms.

Studies reported in 2010 and 2011 in the *Journal of Neuroscience* show that estrogen receptors on neurons influence the structure and activity of synapses in the brain, and these findings may offer clues as to how estrogen influences mood. However, none of these studies provide answers to how and why BD is likely to begin during adolescence and young adulthood. Scientists are now conducting other studies to shed more light on this issue.

There have been fewer studies examining the relationship between androgens, or male hormones, and BD, but scientists do know that when androgens such as testosterone become active during adolescence, this results in changes in brain circuits and structure. For instance, testosterone makes nerve fibers in the frontal lobes of the brain acquire more insulation during adolescence in AMABs, and this allows faster signal transmission. The amygdala and hippocampus both increase in size at this time, too, and scientists believe these changes may contribute to adolescents' increased vulnerability to BD.

Men with BD are more likely to experience mania when their testosterone levels are too high and depression when they are too low. Livestrong, a medical and scientific website, explained:

> *Testosterone may not be a direct cause of the chemical imbalance underlying depression. Low levels of this hormone, however, gives rise to … irritability and a lack of energy. These negative mental and physical factors may lead to an increased breakdown of serotonin in the brain, a state directly linked to depression.*
>
> *High testosterone levels, on the other hand, are more likely to give rise to symptoms of mania. Excessive amounts of available testosterone in the bloodstream can give rise to irritability, aggressiveness … and a desire to act. The extreme energy levels that accompany high testosterone can also distort rational thought processes and lead to irrational decision making …*
>
> *Though there is no direct scientific evidence to suggest that fluctuating testosterone levels have any bearing on clinically diagnosed bipolar disorder,*

> *an imbalance in testosterone could be a factor in bipolar disorder.*[21]

EMOTIONAL TRIGGERS

Many researchers believe that in people with a genetic predisposition to BD, symptoms appear when certain triggering events happen. Some of the events experts believe can be involved are physical, emotional, or sexual abuse, particularly during childhood; sleep disruptions; and drug or alcohol abuse. Scientists, however, have not proven that any of these factors actually cause BD, as stated by the author of *The Bipolar Disorder Survival Guide*:

> *The hypothesis that a person's genetic inheritance or biological vulnerabilities interact with specific environmental conditions to produce bipolar disorder is just that: a hypothesis. To test this hypothesis in a research study, we would have to determine whether children born with a genetic history of bipolar disorder and affected by predisposing environmental conditions are more likely to develop bipolar disorder in adulthood than children with a similar genetic history who have not been affected by these environmental conditions. These long-term studies, which would take many years to complete and are extremely difficult to execute, have not been done.*[22]

Although no specific events have been proven to cause BD, scientists do have strong evidence that some events significantly raise the risk of developing the disorder. Stressful or traumatic events such as a death or illness in the family, a divorce, or abuse can trigger or worsen BD episodes in biologically vulnerable people. Doctors believe such stressors can trigger BD by increasing the body's production of certain chemicals such as the stress hormone cortisol, which then acts to disrupt the brain's chemistry.

Although substance abuse is not considered a direct cause of BD, there is strong evidence that it makes symptoms of this disorder worse. Experts believe substance abuse also interferes with a person's ability to recover after experiencing a manic or depressive episode.

A new baby can be a big trigger for a bipolar episode, either depressive or manic. The change in hormones after giving birth, the reduced sleep while the baby is still waking up during the night, and the sudden and drastic change in lifestyle can all play a role in triggering an episode.

Researchers have found that even positive life changes, such as getting a job promotion, getting married, or having a baby can trigger an episode. One doctor who has studied this process extensively is psychology professor Sheri Johnson of the University of California, Berkeley. Johnson believes inborn abnormalities in parts of the brain that regulate emotional control and planning make the brains of people with BD unable to calm neural circuits known as the behavioral activation and inhibition systems. This lack of control occurs during both positive and negative life changes and can lead to manic or depressive episodes.

Johnson has also proposed that in some cases, bipolar episodes cause life changes, which then trigger more bipolar episodes in an ongoing spiral of events. For instance, an individual in a manic state may become confrontational at work and get fired from their job, which in turn intensifies the manic episode. The patient and their doctors may think the job loss triggered the manic episode, when in reality, the mania caused the job loss. Ongoing research in this area indicates that the interactions between life events and BD may be far more complicated than simple cause-and-effect relationships.

Another known trigger of BD episodes is sleep disruption. Patients report that even one night of going to bed late or getting up early can have serious consequences, leading to rapid cycling or worsening of manic or depressive symptoms. Doctors believe this happens because abnormalities in the biological clock make it difficult for patients to adapt to changing sleep patterns. Many times, life changes such as starting college, getting married, starting or ending a relationship, or having a baby disrupt a person's sleep schedule, and the combination of major life events and sleep loss can cause BD to emerge or worsen.

The complex interactions between life events, genetics, and biochemistry that contribute to causing BD make pinning down the exact causes difficult. Different triggers affect different people in different ways, and ongoing research is attempting to understand what biological factors underlie these differences in individual responses. As scientists understand more and more about these processes, new and better treatments emerge, and experts hope that someday this understanding will also lead to methods of preventing the disorder in vulnerable people.

OLD AND NEW TREATMENTS

Because the causes of bipolar disorder are so complex, effective treatment must address all of the variables. Each patient responds to different therapies in different ways, and often combinations of therapies are the most effective. The majority of BD patients respond well to a combination of talk therapy and a class of medication known as mood stabilizers. However, finding the best treatment combination can be a challenge. It can take months—sometimes even years—to determine the best type of medication, its proper dosage, and the appropriate talk therapy approach to best help a patient find balance.

Although BD is not curable, modern treatments help many patients recover from episodes and remain symptom-free for varying lengths of time. However, in order for any treatment to be effective, it must be ongoing. As Dr. David Miklowitz, the author of *The Bipolar Disorder Survival Guide*, explained, "The nature of bipolar disorder is such that even when you feel better, you still have an underlying biological predisposition to the illness. This predisposition requires you to take medication even when you're feeling well."[23] Many people with BD and other mental illnesses stop taking their medication when they feel better, believing that they are cured—only to have their symptoms return. A 2007 study funded by NIMH found that ongoing treatment significantly reduces the number and severity of relapses, and patients have the best outcomes when they work closely with a psychiatrist and keep their doctor notified of any mood changes so appropriate dosage or drug changes can be made. Many patients find that keeping a daily mood chart or journal to track symptoms is especially helpful in managing an ongoing treatment plan.

MEDICATION

The primary goal of using medication is to correct the chemical imbalances that underlie BD. Different drugs and combinations of drugs work best for different patients, and an individual's response to these medications can change over time. Therefore, ongoing monitoring is essential. Another factor that makes finding the right treatment plan an ongoing and complex process, wrote Miklowitz, is that "doctors have to be constantly updated on which treatments to recommend to which patients, since the accepted treatment guidelines for this disorder change so rapidly."[24]

Most patients require drug treatments for both acute (sudden) episodes and ongoing maintenance control. The medications or dosages used for each of these phases may vary. Ongoing treatment is generally self-administered at home, while acute, severe episodes may require hospitalization with more powerful, faster-acting drugs to stabilize the individual so they can function.

Most of the time, a patient voluntarily enters a psychiatric hospital or goes for outpatient treatment. However, if the patient is an immediate danger to themselves or others or has already committed a crime, a judge can order hospitalization or outpatient treatment. State laws vary on this issue, and some states allow family members and law enforcement personnel more flexibility in forcing treatment on someone who does not want it. This is a controversial subject, since balancing an individual's right to make their own decisions with personal and public safety can be challenging.

MOOD STABILIZERS

The most common medications used for both acute episodes and ongoing therapy are called mood stabilizers. Lithium is the oldest effective mood stabilizer; it was approved in 1970 for use in the United States. Experts are not entirely sure why it works, although they do know that it has an effect on brain chemistry in some way.

Lithium is considered the most effective bipolar treatment, especially for manic episodes. Because someone must take lithium for several weeks before it reaches its full effectiveness, it is better as a long-term maintenance treatment—to reduce the severity and frequency of manic and depressive episodes—rather than an emergency short-term treatment to control the effects of an episode when someone is in the middle of it.

Although lithium is very effective, many people avoid it because it has a negative reputation due to its side effects. Some of the more extreme side effects include seizures, hallucinations, vision problems, muscle weakness, nausea, vomiting, and lack of coordination. However, these are not normal side effects; they are considered signs of an emergency. Too much lithium can cause a condition called lithium toxicity, which can be deadly if ignored. However, it is easily treated if the patient temporarily stops taking lithium or if the dose is reduced. More common side effects include restlessness, dry mouth, thirst, indigestion, brittle hair and nails, and frequent urination.

Doctors must carefully monitor the level of lithium in the blood to ensure that it stays within a very narrow range: high enough to manage BD symptoms, but low enough not to cause other health problems. One of the most severe side effects of lithium is kidney failure. A 2017 study found that people who took lithium for more than 10 years had significant changes in their kidney function, but because their doctors were monitoring them, no one in the study went into fatal kidney failure.

Lithium can also cause major birth defects or heart problems in a developing fetus if taken by a pregnant woman. However, experts say lithium is the safest BD medication to use during pregnancy if medication is essential in a given case. Many medications can cause problems if a woman gets pregnant, so women are advised to talk to their doctors about possible side effects if they become pregnant while taking a certain medication.

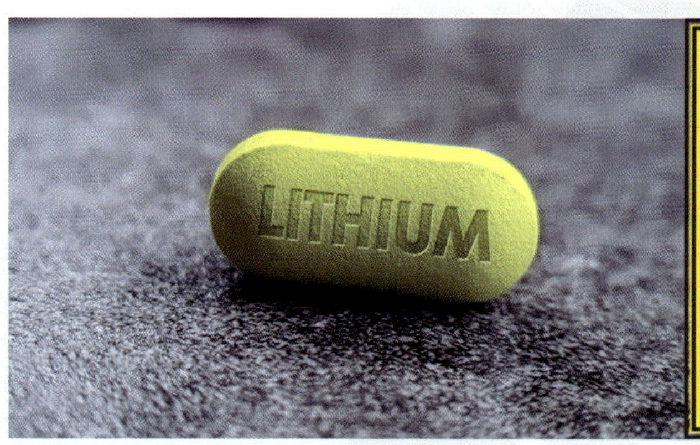

For many years, lithium was considered the best choice for controlling bipolar disorder. However, its use has steadily declined for years due to stigma and concern over its side effects. By 2023, antipsychotics and anticonvulsants were the first choice for prescriptions.

Fear of lithium's side effects has given lithium a stigma, or negative reputation. Doctors say that all medications have some possible side effects, and many doctors and BD patients agree that the benefits of lithium outweigh its negative effects. A British newspaper, the *Guardian,* reported in 2016 that one study found "that only an estimated 10% of those with bipolar disorder use [lithium], mainly because patients fear it will cause loss of personality, weight gain and other problems."[25] The authors of the study said this stigma against lithium comes mainly from the decades before the 1980s, when patients were given too large a dose. They found that when given a proper dose, lithium patients gained less weight than those on other medications and were 40 percent less likely to harm themselves. Since BD has one of the highest risks of suicide of any mental illness, this is an important feature.

Terri Cheney, a BD patient, also believes the mild side effects of properly administered lithium are worth enduring. In an article for *Psychology Today*, she wrote that at one point she missed the highs of her mania:

> *I knew that lithium is my friend. It helps me stay sane, but it also tamps me down. My creativity suffers, exuberance [high energy and cheerfulness] flees, and I experience a certain degree of cognitive dulling—not unbearable, but by no means pleasant, either. And pleasure was all I was after … I longed for my old intensity, even though it wasn't always limited to pleasure … Lithium may be a barrier to joy, but it keeps desperation at bay. The trade-off was worth it, or so I kept on telling myself.*[26]

Cheney was trying to decide whether or not to take her lithium so she could experience her mania again when her best friend called, crying because her daughter had attempted suicide. After they hung up, Cheney wrote that she felt "a wave of relief":

> *Thank God, this time it wasn't me. It wasn't my mother having to make those desperate phone calls late at night. Please, can you help me? Please, can you help her? I was here, safe at home, pills in hand. And that's when it hit me: true joy isn't a flood of sensory bliss. It is, quite simply, a lack of drama. Gratefully, I swallowed my lithium and turned off the light.*[27]

TAILORING MEDICATIONS

Although lithium is a proven treatment for many BD patients, it is less effective for those with rapid cycling, mixed states, or co-occurring substance abuse. Lithium is also far more effective in reducing the number of manic episodes than it is in treating depression. Other mood stabilizers used to treat BD are anticonvulsant drugs originally developed to treat epilepsy. Valproic acid, also known as valproate or divalproex (or by the brand name Depakote) is the most widely used in this class. It works by reducing activity of the enzyme known as protein kinase C and increasing the activity of the neurotransmitter GABA, which calms neuron firing. Since everyone's body chemistry is different, some people find that valproate controls their symptoms as effectively as lithium without the issue of breaking down the kidneys. However, valproate comes with its own set of side effects, which may include drowsiness, dizziness, diarrhea, constipation, heartburn, runny nose, and liver or pancreas problems. It can also raise levels of the male hormone testosterone in both sexes, and this can lead to polycystic ovary syndrome (PCOS) in women who begin taking the drug before age 20. PCOS involves eggs turning into fluid-filled cysts that can disrupt menstruation and lead to obesity and excess body hair.

Other anticonvulsants approved to treat BD include lamotrigine (Lamictal), gabapentin (Neurontin), topiramate (Topamax), carbamazepine (Tegretol), and oxcarbazepine (Trileptal). Each of these help varying types of BD, and some are more effective at reducing either mania or depression symptoms, as opposed to reducing both. For example, studies performed in 2003, 2004, and 2009 have shown lamotrigine to be more effective than lithium in preventing depressive relapses, rapid cycling, and mixed states. Some of these medications can be less effective than lithium or valproate, but they generally do help many patients who cannot tolerate those drugs. When used together with lithium, they can be more effective at treating both mood states. Many people need a combination of drugs because there are no currently available drugs to treat all aspects of BD.

ALL BODIES ARE DIFFERENT

Everyone reacts differently to different medications and different doses. Because of this, it can take some experimentation to find out what works best for an individual. Patients should talk to their doctor about how a particular medication makes them feel; a good doctor will listen and work with them to figure out how to adjust the medication so that it is working effectively with as few side effects as possible. Patients are within their rights to find a new doctor if their current doctor tells them they are imagining the side effects or that there is only one option for them.

In a 2017 article for the *New York Times*, BD patient Jaime Lowe wrote about how two different versions of Depakote affected her in wildly different ways:

> *I refilled my prescription and noticed that the pills were slightly different from the month before … Though both were generic, one was known as Depakote D.R. (for delayed release), the other as Depakote E.R. (for extended release). I asked my pharmacist if there was a difference and he said, no, they are the same chemical makeup. It turns out there are studies that claim that the two different forms of Depakote are interchangeable …*
>
> *Within a day of taking the Depakote D.R., I was bloated again—angry, irritated, fat-feeling, hair-losing and sobbing. I was increasing the dose at the same time, so I assumed that my symptoms were just a reaction to the amount I was taking … In October 2016, I refilled my prescription again. And within 24 hours, I felt better. This time the bottle said "Depakote E.R." Two days later, I still had side effects, but they were mild by comparison … I was responding well to one form of Depakote but not to another, yet my pharmacist had sent me home assuring me they were interchangeable. According to my body, they are not.*[1]

According to Lowe's psychiatrist, many doctors are educated about a drug's effects by the pharmaceutical companies that sell them, so their knowledge may have gaps. This is why it is important for doctors and patients to have open communication about the ways a drug is affecting the individual.

1. Jaime Lowe, "The Wrong Pill Can Play with Your Mind," *New York Times*, September 30, 2017. www.nytimes.com/2017/09/30/opinion/sunday/bipolar-medication-depakote-lithium-.html.

All anticonvulsants can cause drowsiness, nausea, blurry vision, memory loss, loss of coordination, and liver disease. In addition, all carry a warning that they may increase suicidal thoughts and can cause a life-threatening rash called Stevens-Johnson syndrome.

EFFECTIVE AND INEFFECTIVE MEDICATIONS

It may seem logical that using antidepressants along with mood stabilizers would be effective in treating BD, but this is often not the case. In general, antidepressants are not nearly as effective in helping depressed bipolar patients as they are for treating unipolar depression. Some studies, including a 2007 study reported in the *New England Journal of Medicine*, have found "no evidence that treatment with a mood stabilizer and an antidepressant confers a benefit over treatment with a mood stabilizer alone."[28] Other studies, however, have found that antidepressants can help manage depressive episodes far better than mood stabilizers do, so there is controversy among doctors about whether or not to prescribe antidepressants for BD.

The fact that some antidepressants trigger mania in depressed BD patients also makes many physicians hesitant to prescribe them. Some studies have concluded that antidepressants trigger mania only when they are used by themselves in bipolar patients, while other studies have found that this can happen even when they are used along with mood stabilizers.

When they are used, antidepressants known as selective serotonin reuptake inhibitors (SSRIs), including fluoxetine (Prozac), paroxetine (Paxil), and sertraline (Zoloft), are among the most popular. Also frequently prescribed are serotonin-norepinephrine reuptake inhibitors (SNRIs), which act on both of these neurotransmitters (serotonin and norepinephrine). These include venlafaxine (Effexor) and duloxetine (Cymbalta). Older antidepressants called tricyclic antidepressants and monoamine oxidase inhibitors (MAOIs) are also effective for some patients, but they are less often prescribed because they have harsher side effects. Additionally, people who take MAOIs cannot eat certain foods that react in a potentially deadly way with the drug, such as aged cheeses, pepperoni, sour cream, avocados, and soy sauce. This strict diet can be difficult for people to follow, especially if they are unaware that one of the items they must avoid is in the ingredients of a food.

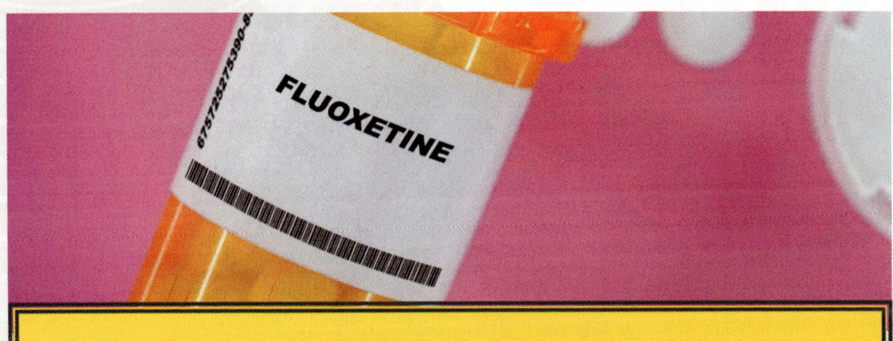

Antidepressants such as fluoxetine (also called Prozac) work very well for unipolar depression. However, with bipolar disorder, they can trigger a manic episode.

All antidepressants can potentially cause nausea, sleeplessness, and headaches, although the newer drugs are less likely to have serious side effects. Antidepressants can also trigger or worsen thoughts of suicide, especially in adolescents.

Another type of medication often used to treat BD is atypical antipsychotics. "Atypical" refers to the fact that these drugs are distinct from older, or conventional, antipsychotics. Antipsychotics primarily help lessen psychotic symptoms, but they are also effective in quickly controlling severe mania, depression, or mixed episodes. One of the most effective is olanzapine (Zyprexa), which is approved by the U.S. Food and Drug Administration (FDA) to be used for long-term maintenance as well as to treat manic episodes and episodes with mixed features. It is not approved to treat depressive episodes, but some patients may find it helpful in this area as well. When a doctor prescribes a medication for something it is not approved by the FDA to treat, it is called prescribing off-label. The medication has still gone through the required safety testing; FDA approval simply means that studies show a particular drug to be effective at treating a particular illness or symptom in a large population. A smaller population may find that a particular drug treats a particular symptom for them but not for many other people. In this case, their doctor can prescribe the drug for them off-label.

Other commonly used antipsychotics include aripiprazole (Abilify), quetiapine (Seroquel), and risperidone (Risperdal). All can cause weight gain, diabetes, heart disease, drowsiness, dizziness, blurred vision, skin rashes, and menstrual problems. Some side effects lessen over time, but some do not. Long-term use of antipsychotics, defined as three months or more, can also lead to uncontrollable twitching known as tardive dyskinesia, which can become permanent if ignored. For this reason, it is important for patients to let their doctor know immediately if they start to get symptoms so their dose can be lowered or they can be switched to a different medication.

A newer combination pill known as Symbyax contains Zyprexa and Prozac. In studies, patients taking Symbyax experienced greater improvement in their depression than patients taking a placebo, or fake treatment. This improvement stayed noticeable over the full course of eight-week studies.

PROBLEMS WITH MEDICATIONS

Besides the side effects that can make patients reluctant to take BD drugs, other safety issues exist. Not all BD medications approved for adults are also approved for use in children and adolescents, since side effects, safety, and effectiveness in young people may differ from those in adults. No BD drugs are approved for children under age 10. Several atypical antipsychotics are approved for children ages 10 to 17, and lithium is approved for ages 12 to 17. However, even for young adults who fall between the ages of 10 and 18, medication is not always an easy choice. At these ages, the body is still developing, so BD drugs can have unpredictable side effects. A 2012 study published in the *Archives of Pediatrics and Adolescent Medicine* found that only 14 percent of teens who have a mental disorder take medication.

Balancing the needs of the body with the needs of the mind is tricky, but many medical professionals believe the benefits of taking BD medication outweigh the risks. According to psychiatrist Janet Wozniak, "I understand the reason why a parent would be afraid to medicate their child … But parents also need to consider that there may be a downside to not medicating and missing an opportunity to interrupt the course of a serious illness ... Not medicating may also carry with it risks."[29] These risks include an interruption in education, which can have a serious effect on a person's later life, and suicide. According to the National Alliance on Mental Illness (NAMI), "Half of students with mental illness ages 14 and older drop out of high school, the highest rate of other groups with disabilities."[30] Mental illness, including BD, can make it difficult for someone to concentrate on schoolwork and make it hard to fit in with their peers, which causes many people with untreated mental illnesses to choose to stop attending altogether.

Doctors and pharmacists are a crucial part of controlling bipolar disorder. Taking or stopping medication without their advice and supervision can cause serious problems.

The fact that most BD drugs given to patients for ongoing treatment take a while to start working is another issue of concern to many patients. Some drugs take days or even weeks to show results, and many people become impatient and stop taking them. Experts say this is not a good idea. Patients should always consult their doctor before starting or stopping any medication.

Studies show that many BD patients stop taking their prescribed medications at some point for other reasons too. The most common reason is called anosognosia, which is a medical word that means the person has a lack of awareness about their disease. In other words, the patient may think their BD symptoms are normal behaviors that do not need to be addressed with medication or that improved symptoms mean their BD has been cured for good. Another common reason why people stop taking their medication is that they have a poor relationship with their psychiatrist. If they do not trust their psychiatrist for any reason—even a seemingly small one, such as that the psychiatrist has a condescending tone when they speak to them—they are less likely to trust the psychiatrist's advice on medication matters. The psychiatrist may be a good doctor, but personality is an important factor to consider. Some personality types naturally clash, and a patient must find a doctor whose personality fits well with their own. People who do not like or trust their psychiatrist should seek a new one.

Other important issues are the cost of medication and frustration with apparent lack of improvement. Some people are unaware that they might need to experiment to find the right combination of medications that control their symptoms, so if they are on a drug regimen that is not working for them or causes unbearable side effects, they might simply stop taking their medication rather than trying something else. Enjoyment of manic episodes, as Cheney wrote about, is also a factor for people with BD. The urge to feel that kind of high again can be very tempting, which is why a strong support network of family, friends, and mental health professionals is crucial.

Because of safety concerns, side effects, or ineffectiveness of conventional drug therapy, some patients try alternative therapies, such as herbal or other natural products. Others take these natural remedies together with medication. Doctors say some of these products may be harmless, but others are dangerous, especially if combined with certain medications. Additionally, while some patients may find that they work, there have been few scientific studies done on their effectiveness.

Generally, as long as a treatment is not actively harming a patient, there is no problem with trying it, but all natural remedies should be discussed with a doctor first. For example, the herb rhodiola has mild anti-stress and antidepressant properties and can also help boost a person's energy. Because it is much milder than a medical antidepressant, it has fewer side effects, but it is also less effective at decreasing depression, so it is typically used in combination with other medications. St. John's wort, in contrast, is an herb with stronger antidepressant properties, but like medical antidepressants, it can cause bipolar patients to cycle from depression to mania. It can also interact with other BD medications in unpredictable ways. Herbal remedies are also not regulated by the FDA, and manufacturers and alternative practitioners often make exaggerated claims. The strength of the dose and the ingredients on the label also may not always be accurate, so people should use caution and look for certified brands that are more likely to be trustworthy.

TALKING IT OUT

Whichever medications prove to be best for a particular patient, research shows that combining therapy with medication is more effective than either alone. Therapy generally combines talking about problems with behavior modification. It can be administered by a psychiatrist, psychologist (professional with a Ph.D. in clinical psychology who is licensed to provide psychotherapy but not to prescribe drugs), social worker, counselor, or psychiatric nurse. Therapies that are most effective are ones that help patients recognize the patterns that occur within their BD, manage stress to reduce manic and depressive episodes, and practice self-care.

One common type of therapy is cognitive behavioral therapy (CBT). This type of therapy helps patients change negative thought and behavior patterns by recognizing how viewing themselves in a negative light leads to harmful emotions and behaviors.

As BD patient Denise Krischke wrote:

When the medications allowed me to achieve some sort of balance, a therapist helped to reshape negative thoughts and behaviors, experienced and unintentionally developed into habits during the darkest times. Life takes on a whole new perspective once the chemical monsters are fought. One then has to deal with the internal struggle of having a mental illness and the public's perception of the disorder while attempting to become well.[31]

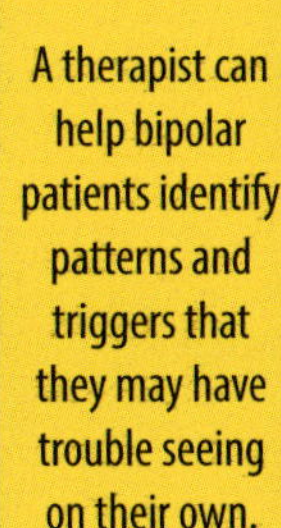

A therapist can help bipolar patients identify patterns and triggers that they may have trouble seeing on their own.

While CBT generally involves only the patient and their therapist, family-focused therapy helps family members and patients work together to develop coping strategies and action plans for dealing with episodes. A similar form of therapy called interpersonal and social rhythm therapy (IPSRT) helps patients learn to improve relationships with others and to establish a regular sleep schedule to reduce and prevent episodes.

BD patients who also have substance abuse problems may need inpatient or outpatient counseling or rehabilitation to treat the substance abuse. "Inpatient" means they check into a facility where they can have round-the-clock care, while "outpatient" means they live at home but attend sessions, either alone or with a group, on a weekly or semi-weekly basis. Some patients benefit from groups such as Alcoholics Anonymous (AA) or from group therapy in a clinic. According to the Depression and Bipolar Support Alliance (DBSA), not treating substance abuse significantly reduces the effectiveness of any BD treatment. The DBSA also recommends that patients be careful about which substance abuse treatment program they choose, since some encourage people to stop taking all drugs, even prescribed ones:

> *Some drug and alcohol recovery groups may believe that you can't be clean and sober if you take medications prescribed by a doctor. This belief is just plain wrong. Medication for your mood disorder is no different than medication for another illness such as asthma, high blood pressure or diabetes. If your recovery group challenges your use of medication, it is probably best for you to become part of another group that understands the concept of dual diagnosis.*[32]

A CONTROVERSIAL THERAPY

Some people's BD is highly resistant to the most common forms of treatment. In cases where medication and therapy are ineffective, a patient may be given electroconvulsive therapy (ECT). This is when a psychiatrist gives the patient a muscle relaxant and general anesthesia, then an electric shock lasting 30 to 90 seconds is administered to the head through electrodes attached to the scalp. This produces a seizure that lasts about a minute. Most patients recover within 15 minutes.

ECT is generally given three times per week for two to four weeks. However, some BD patients require ongoing ECT, while others need only occasional follow-up treatments. Doctors believe ECT works to treat BD by changing a patient's brain chemistry.

ECT has been controversial because of movies and books such as *One Flew Over the Cuckoo's Nest*, in which it is depicted as abusive. Doctors say that while it is true that older forms of ECT were extremely unpleasant for patients, had serious side effects, and were often used as a form of punishment to keep patients in mental hospitals in line, modern technology and better knowledge of the appropriate length and strength of the shock has made ECT a tolerable, safe, and fast-acting treatment for people who find other treatments to be ineffective.

The Mayo Clinic explained:

> *Much of the stigma attached to electroconvulsive therapy is based on early treatments in which high doses of electricity were administered without anesthesia, leading to memory loss, fractured bones and other serious side effects. ECT is much safer today … It now uses electrical currents given in a controlled setting to achieve the most benefit with the fewest possible risks.*[33]

Modern ECT may still cause mild side effects such as confusion, temporary memory loss, nausea, headache, muscle spasms, and increased blood pressure, but these effects generally go away quickly. Many patients, such as the late Carrie Fisher—a spokesperson for the BD community who was best known for her role as Princess Leia in the *Star Wars* movies—have credited ECT with helping them emerge from severe bipolar episodes for which nothing else was effective. Experts point out that ECT is also safer for pregnant women than BD medications are.

BD cannot be cured, and relapses may happen regardless of what treatment someone is on. However, with careful management and open communication between doctors and patients, the majority of people with BD can experience long stretches of time with no life-altering symptoms.

MANAGING BD

Managing bipolar disorder is often difficult, especially when someone is stil trying to find the combination of therapies that work best for them. It can be a challenge for their loved ones as well. However, when friends and families work to better understand the disease, they can develop coping methods and help their loved ones recognize the signs of an oncoming mood episode. The guidance of a medical professional is also extremely valuable in helping families get educated and involved in treatment. Living with any chronic illness can be overwhelming, but studies have shown conclusively that patients with strong support systems have better treatment outcomes than those who do not.

For many, receiving a diagnosis and getting treatment is a reassuring, positive step. Denise Krischke, for example, wrote that after experiencing undiagnosed symptoms since childhood, her diagnosis at age 28 "was a blessing to me and my husband, because we finally had a name for the out of control behaviors that had overtaken me."[34]

For others, however, the process of seeking help is filled with anger or denial that anything is wrong. The good feelings associated with mania, combined with other factors unique to BD, can make this process especially difficult. Many people with mental illnesses, especially BD, wonder, "How do you know what is really your illness and what is your 'self' or your personality (your habits, attitudes, and styles of relating to others)?"[35] Someone with anosognosia generally believes their BD symptoms are just who they are as a person and that they do not need treatment. According to the Treatment Advocacy Center, an organization that works to eliminate the barriers to mental health treatment, anosognosia is "the single largest reason why people with schizophrenia or bipolar disorder refuse medications or do not seek treatment. Without awareness of the illness, refusing treatment appears rational, no matter how clear the need for treatment might be to others."[36] About 40 percent of BD patients have this symptom.

Unfortunately, when BD remains uncontrolled, it can cause issues not only for the patient but for those around them. Many people struggle with deciding whether to end a relationship with a person whose behavior has become unpleasant. When a person with BD denies that they are ill and refuses to seek help, this can push a spouse or partner to decide not to stay, or family members to reduce or cut contact.

OPENING UP

Another aspect of BD that makes accepting and coping with the disease difficult is the stigma of mental illness. At one time, families hid mentally ill people at home or in institutions out of shame, and seeking help was considered embarrassing because then everyone would find out. Today, mental illnesses are talked about and tolerated more, in large part because scientists have discovered biological causes that make others more willing to view these conditions as diseases rather than as weaknesses of character. Additionally, famous people who have been willing to come forward and open up about their personal struggles have shown a wide audience that even people who appear to have perfect lives can still struggle with mental

People who are uninformed about BD may fear people who have it, which makes it hard for BD patients to develop the strong support network that makes managing the disorder easier.

illness. However, stigma still exists and often leads to preconceived notions about "crazy" people—and even to obvious discrimination.

Many people still view someone with BD as naturally violent, angry, and dangerous. The media reinforces this view; studies of movies and TV shows have shown that crime is the most common theme in stories of mental illness. However, in reality, people with mental illnesses are far more likely to be the victims of crime than the perpetrators. While some patients with mental illness do have anger problems or violent tendencies, most do not. Even so, the stigma against them can result in others avoiding or refusing to hire or rent to a person with BD, even if the person has never shown any signs of being dangerous. Although discrimination in housing or employment is illegal, it happens sometimes anyway. Many patients avoid seeking treatment or telling others about their illness for these reasons, hoping that if they pretend nothing is wrong, no one will guess the truth. However, the effects of untreated manic and depressive episodes generally make the reality of the illness impossible to hide.

Other ways the media reinforces stigma is by showing people with BD as unpredictable, with moods that change within minutes. A bipolar character on TV may be shown screaming and crying one second, then laughing the next. In reality, however, bipolar cycles take weeks or months to complete, and there may be long stretches of time where the person is not showing symptoms. Even rapid cycling does not cause someone with BD to change their mood in an instant.

People sometimes use "bipolar" as an insult toward a person who changes their mind quickly, acts moody, or gets upset easily. However, in most cases, the person being described is simply exhibiting normal mood changes. Misuse of the word this way falsely makes people believe BD is not serious and can be hurtful to those who have the disorder. As BD patient Emily Reynolds explained:

> *I know people don't mean to do it and it's thoughtlessness rather than spite, but it just wounds me a little bit every time and makes me feel I can't trust that person … [When] people throw around "I feel so manic" or "he's so bipolar," I just feel awkward about my diagnosis. Even with my level of willingness to talk about it, I feel small and awkard.*[37]

Additionally, most people with normal moods can control them with some effort. This is not true of mental illness. Linking these two creates a false idea that anyone with a mental illness can just "snap out of it," when in reality, it is not that easy. Using the name of a mental illness as an insult creates a situation called negative evaluation, according to Dr. Zsofia Demjen: "When people say that, they don't mean the person is clinically ill. They mean their behavior isn't seen as positive. And again, if you take the idea that words acquire and change meaning, then bipolar … acquires this negative association."[38]

This causes BD patients as well as those around them to see the disorder as something that is naturally bad, which can turn into seeing the person themselves as bad for having the disorder. If people think more carefully before they use the name of a mental illness to describe someone who is not mentally ill, they can keep the word from losing its true meaning and becoming an insult. As journalist Hannah Ewens wrote on the website Vice, "It's not about taking over language and deciding who can say what. It's about having a word to express to people who don't understand what is affecting us."[39]

CHANGING MINDS

Advocacy groups such as NAMI and DBSA, along with affected individuals, work to get rid of the stigma surrounding BD by educating the public about the disease and pointing out that people with BD

BAD BEHAVIOR

Kanye West has been the topic of much controversy in recent years. He has made anti-Semitic, or anti-Jewish, remarks online; he has attacked his former wife, Kim Kardashian, on social media and encouraged his fans to do the same; and, although he is Black, he has made racist remarks against Black people as a whole. West has also been diagnosed with bipolar disorder, which he called his "superpower" in a song called "Yikes." West's fans have frequently defended his behavior, especially when West made it known that he had stopped taking his BD medication because he felt it affected his creativity.

(In 2025, West stated that his bipolar diagnosis was a mistake and that he is actually autistic. It is unclear whether this claim is true; a person can have both BD and autism at the same time, but BD is difficult to diagnose and can appear similar to other conditions, including autism.)

Although BD can make people behave erratically, it does not affect their beliefs, nor does it excuse bad behavior toward others. Mental illness and neurodivergence may make it difficult for someone to control what they say, but neither BD nor autism makes a person prejudiced or abusive. Using BD or autism to excuse bad behavior gives people with these conditions a bad reputation and also gives people a way to avoid taking accountability for their harmful words and actions.

are a diverse group. These advocates also hope that less stigma will lead to more patients being willing to seek and stick with treatment. One vocal advocate was author and actress Carrie Fisher. Fisher publicly discussed her battle with BD, often using humor to educate people. In one interview, Fisher said, "Bipolar disorder is a mood system that functions like the weather. It's independent of the things that happen in your life … I get awards all the time for being mentally ill. I'm a shoo-in because there's no swimsuit competition."[40] In April 2018, singer Mariah Carey announced that she had been diagnosed with bipolar II in 2001. She said it took her years to admit it, even to herself, because of the stigma surrounding it. After getting treatment in the form of medication and therapy, she felt good enough about herself to talk about it publicly, which she hopes will help reduce the stigma further. Other celebrities who have recently opened up about their BD diagnoses include Selena Gomez and Halsey.

Selena Gomez is one celebrity who has opened up about her bipolar disorder diagnosis.

Advocacy groups and individuals have also made progress in encouraging the media to accurately portray people with BD in an effort to cut down on stereotypes and misconceptions. In 2009, for example, the Broadway musical *Next to Normal*, which depicted a woman with BD, won rave reviews and three Tony Awards. Composer Tom Kitt stated in an interview with *bp* magazine that audiences responded well because he and lyricist Brian Yorkey worked hard to make the musical accurate and relatable. They spoke with many BD patients, as well as with psychiatrists and psychologists, while researching the musical. "We both have had experience with bipolar in our own lives and we saw that creating a musical about bipolar was a new way to pull the audience in. We feel the show is filled with empathy and a mixture of sadness, hope, and reality,"[41] he said.

In 2017, comedian Maria Bamford's TV show *Lady Dynamite* premiered and was highly praised for its realistic portrayal of the pain of mental illness and how the struggle with BD can coexist with hope and creativity. The show is loosely based on Bamford's real-life struggle with BD, including hospitalization following a suicide attempt. The second season shows her learning to put her mental health first, while showing how her illness has impacted her life and career.

The TV show *Euphoria* has also shown a realistic, although less hopeful, view of someone with bipolar disorder. Zendaya's character, Rue Bennet, struggles throughout the show with multiple mental illnesses, including BD. Because she is not receiving the proper treatment, she self-medicates with drugs and alcohol, giving her even more problems to deal with. *Euphoria* shows the harsh reality of living with unregulated BD when a person does not have a strong support network.

A BALANCING ACT

Doctors say patients who accept the fact that they have a chronic disease and that they must make changes in their lives to manage it have the best quality of life. By accepting the disease, experts say, patients take some control.

A teen named Michelle, for instance, refused to accept her condition or to take her prescribed medications for several years after her diagnosis at age 12. She was hospitalized repeatedly and finally realized that she would be better off if she stuck with a treatment plan. Her life improved dramatically, and she even started seeing some positive aspects of having a serious illness. She wrote:

> *I learned life lessons at a young age that I will know forever. Some people don't learn these lessons until they're much older. Some people never learn them. One of my closest friends also has bipolar disorder. He always tells me to think of it as a gift and not something bad because it helps you look at life in different ways. With this illness you see things you never would have otherwise.*[42]

In addition to accepting and treating BD, doctors recommend that patients also take steps to live a healthier lifestyle overall. Although BD is not a result of poor health, many people—even those without a mental disorder—find that they feel their best when they make healthy lifestyle choices. Practicing relaxation techniques such as yoga or tai chi, moving their body, and eating a well-balanced diet not only improve physical health but also help people cope by promoting positive changes in brain chemistry. Doctors say that avoiding excessive amounts of sugar, caffeine, and alcohol is especially important in helping regulate mood. People with BD who work in jobs that require irregular hours and a lot of travel also do better

Mindfulness is an important tool for managing mental illnesses as well as general, everyday forms of stress.

if they switch to positions with consistent hours that allow them to keep a regular sleep schedule.

A STRONG SUPPORT NETWORK

Having adequate family and social support can also help patients cope and live fully, and experts advise ending or improving stressful relationships and not associating with people who are a negative influence. Another positive step is encouraging family members and friends to educate themselves about BD and to actively participate in an ongoing action plan so they can reinforce the patient's efforts to manage their illness.

When the patient and family sit down to discuss past episodes and pinpoint early signs that can reveal an approaching episode, this allows them to develop a plan to notify the patient's physician and take other steps to prevent the episode from spiraling out of control. Family members and close friends learn to look for common early signs of mania that may include sleep disturbances, making overly ambitious plans, talking nonstop, or becoming confrontational. Signs of impending depression can be less obvious but may include negative thoughts, sadness, tiredness, withdrawing from social situations, and having trouble sleeping and concentrating.

For some patients, having a family member help keep track of events that consistently come before an episode can also help with prevention. These events may include an important test at school, staying up late with friends, or a confrontation with a parent or guardian. Once the patient and family member document the triggering events, a therapist can then help the patient develop methods of avoiding or coping with such situations.

Many people with BD and their families also draw up written contracts that give certain family

Parents are an important part of a person's support network. Parents of people who have been diagnosed with BD should take steps to educate themselves about the disorder in general and how it affects their child in particular.

members permission to take steps to rein in the patient's behavior if their anosognosia makes them unable to see that they are about to do regrettable things. The person with BD can give their family member permission to take away their credit cards and checkbook, take them to the psychiatrist even if they do not want to go, or forbid them to make life-changing decisions such as changing jobs, getting married or divorced, or moving. Although a pre-manic person may not see the need for such restrictions, many find that previously signing a contract prevents unfortunate consequences later.

CONNECTING WITH OTHERS

Many patients and families find that participating in local or online support groups is also helpful for recognizing early signs of episodes as well as for coping in general. Support groups consist of individuals dealing with the same illness and its problems. Some are led by a facilitator, while others meet more informally to share information and compassion. Because group members understand what others with BD are going through, they are often very helpful in alerting people about impending episodes and offering coping strategies.

Many people find that reaching out to help others through support groups, advocacy organizations, or other avenues also improves their own lives.

Andy Behrman, for example, wrote *Electroboy: A Memory of Mania* to help others by sharing his experiences with BD and found he developed a sense of

HELPFUL AND UNHELPFUL

The Depression and Bipolar Support Alliance offered the following advice to BD patients' family members and friends who wish to be helpful:

What you can say that helps:

- *You are not alone in this. I'm here for you.*
- *I understand you have a real illness and that's what causes these thoughts and feelings.*
- *You may not believe it now, but the way you're feeling will change.*
- *I may not be able to understand exactly how you feel, but I care about you and want to help.*
- *When you want to give up, tell yourself you will hold on for just one more day, hour, minute—whatever you can manage.*
- *You are important to me. Your life is important to me.*
- *Tell me what I can do now to help you.*
- *I am here for you. We will get through this together.*

What you should avoid saying:

- *It's all in your head.*
- *We all go through times like this.*
- *You'll be fine. Stop worrying.*
- *Look on the bright side.*
- *You have so much to live for, why do you want to die?*
- *I can't do anything about your situation.*
- *Just snap out of it.*
- *Stop acting crazy.*
- *What's wrong with you?*
- *Shouldn't you be better by now?*[1]

1. "Helping Someone with a Mood Disorder," Depression and Bipolar Support Alliance. www.dbsalliance.org/site/PageServer?pagename=about_helping.

Support groups can be helpful both for BD patients and their families.

pride from serving as a source of hope for others. He wrote:

> *I thought that my sharing my story, a very personal story, would bring people out of the closet to seek treatment, help family members in understanding their loved ones, and also help mental healthcare professionals in treating their patients … Passing on my knowledge of my coping skills is the most important thing that I can do with my life.*[43]

Before achieving stability, Behrman endured being misdiagnosed for 10 years, trying nearly 40 different medications, undergoing ECT, losing his job as a public relations agent and art dealer, and going to jail for counterfeiting art while in a manic state. His story and the stories of others who live successfully with BD give many patients hope.

Stories like Behrman's and those of celebrities such as Selena Gomez inspire people with BD to believe that they can still achieve great things, even with their diagnosis. However, experts and people affected by BD agree that there is still much to do in the future before the personal and societal impact of bipolar disorder can be diminished.

EMERGING RESEARCH

Although BD treatment has come a long way, experts agree there is still much to learn. Their aim is to lessen the suffering of those with the disorder and to diminish the negative social effects so that BD patients can lead better lives. In addition to the emotional and financial costs of the disorder to individuals, government agencies, and insurance companies, people with BD are also at an increased risk of developing other serious illnesses, such as heart disease, stroke, diabetes, and certain cancers.

NEW THERAPY OPTIONS

Some researchers believe a type of therapy called behavioral interpersonal psychotherapy could help prevent BD or allow early detection of BD in teens who have a parent with the disease. One 2015 meta-study (a study of many other studies) found that the earlier therapy is applied and the more it is tailored to address the individual's unique situation, the better effect it has on a person's life.

The researchers in this meta-study also noted that most studies have been done on patients with bipolar I. However, behavioral interpersonal psychotherapy has shown some promise as a potential treatment for bipolar II as well and could potentially be used to treat it exclusively with therapy (as opposed to treating it with medication and therapy combined).

When used with medication, this type of therapy has been shown to reduce recovery time after a depressive episode for patients with bipolar I and II. It has also shown some improvement in patients' ability to function socially and at work. These results are promising, but more studies are needed to evaluate the adjustments made to tailor the therapy to address the challenges of BD.

MORE RESEARCH

In addition to improving therapy for BD, many scientists are attempting to better understand the causes of BD in hopes of improving treatments and quality of life for patients. Some studies are searching for more gene mutations that are linked to BD. Researchers believe that finding a complete set of genes that contribute to a genetic predisposition can then lead to a better understanding of how the chemicals produced as a result of instructions from these genes interact to increase someone's risk of developing BD.

Related studies are evaluating how different neurotransmitters contribute to BD. Previous research has documented how serotonin, norepinephrine, glutamate, GABA, and several other neurotransmitters play a role, and NIMH research has used fMRI to see how the neurotransmitter acetylcholine affects behavior and thought patterns in people with the illness. Acetylcholine is known to affect memory and attention, and scientists believe that areas in the brain that produce and respond to acetylcholine may become overly sensitive during depressive episodes. Researchers have found that the drug scopolamine, which diminishes acetylcholine activity, helps reduce depression with less threat of causing a manic or hypomanic episode than antidepressants. It also works much faster than SSRIs, providing relief from depression in a matter of hours rather than weeks. However, it is approved by the FDA to treat motion sickness, not depression, so it is not marketed as a BD treatment. Some doctors prescribe it to their BD patients off-label.

Other studies at several medical centers are using MRI to assess differences in the brains of people with BD, those with a genetic predisposition to BD but no signs of illness, and healthy control subjects. Brain imaging is also being used to assess how BD medications correct the brain abnormalities seen in patients.

DEVELOPING NEW TREATMENTS

One goal of furthering an understanding of the brain changes that cause BD is to develop treatments that specifically target these areas. Experts believe that this increased understanding may make new therapies more tolerable than existing treatments are. Researchers are focusing on testing new drugs and nondrug therapies, assessing which drug combinations are most effective, and evaluating the safety of drug treatments for the rapidly expanding population of children with BD. However, one limitation of the studies that have been done so far is that many of them are small. This means it is unclear how helpful some of the therapies being tested will be to a large portion of people with BD. In other words, even the most cutting-edge treatments may not work for most people, and there will still be a large trial-and-error component to finding the right treatment for each individual patient.

Investigators test drugs and other therapies in clinical trials by dividing patients into an experimental and a control group. Those in the experimental group receive the treatment being tested, while those in the control group receive a placebo, or a fake that looks like the real thing. This allows scientists to determine whether any improvements are due to the treatment itself or to the patient's expectation of success.

One drug being tested is ketamine, which is currently approved as an anesthetic for human and veterinary medicine. Ketamine is also sometimes used illegally as a recreational drug because of its ability to induce hallucinations and a dreamlike state. A preliminary study on a small number of bipolar patients indicated that ketamine administered by a doctor can be a fast-acting antidepressant in people for whom other treatments have been unsuccessful. According to an article on the news website Reuters:

> *The 18 patients in the study had tried an average of seven different drugs for treating their bipolar illness, and were still severely depressed; 55 percent had failed electroconvulsive therapy (ECT), or shock treatment. But within 40 minutes of receiving a ketamine injection, their depressive symptoms improved; the effect persisted for at least three days.*[44]

However, the effects of ketamine do not last very long, so researchers are experimenting with combining ketamine and other drugs to prolong the effect. In one small 2015 study, eight patients whose BD did not respond to other existing treatments were given a combination of ketamine and a drug called D-cycloserine. The participants reported a 50 percent decrease in deprcssion symptoms and a 75 percent decrease in suicidal feelings, and these effects lasted throughout the eight weeks of the study. In contrast, the effects of ketamine alone often fade within a week.

In other research on combinations of drugs, scientists are testing various combinations of mood stabilizers, antidepressants, anticonvulsants, and antipsychotics to figure out whether combining these medications reduces the number of relapses and controls mood episodes more than each drug alone does. Other new drug combinations aim to reduce certain side effects.

For example, a medication called Lybalvi combines an atypical antipsychotic with a drug called an opioid receptor antagonist, which is generally used to help patients recover from opioid addiction. The antipsychotic is known to cause weight gain, and the opioid receptor antagonist helps the body regulate weight. By combining the two, BD patients can get the benefits of the antipsychotic without the side effect of weight gain, which can be a major reason why people stop taking mental health medications.

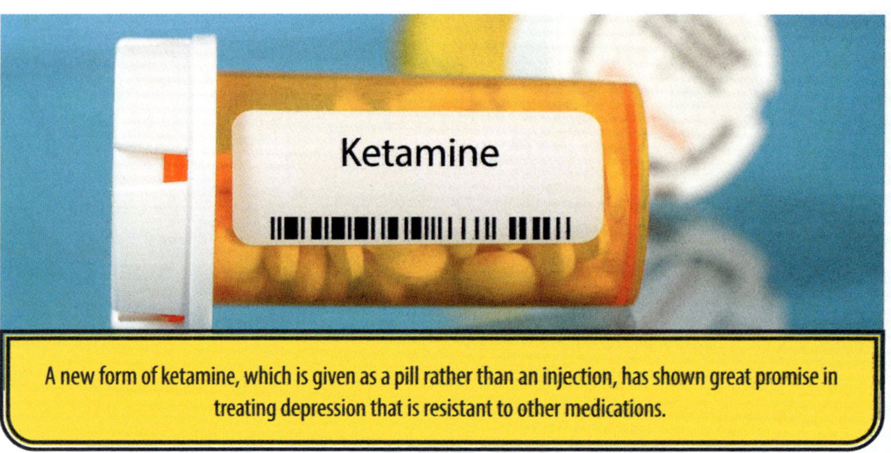

A new form of ketamine, which is given as a pill rather than an injection, has shown great promise in treating depression that is resistant to other medications.

Since drugs can have different effects in children and adolescents than they do in adults, additional studies are trying to determine safe and effective doses of BD drugs that have been approved for adults when these medications are given to children. According to the National Institutes of Health Clinical Center, "Pediatric BD is often difficult to treat; children may respond only partially to the medications now available or have too many side effects to tolerate them."[45]

ALTERNATIVE MEDICINE

Scientists are also testing the safety and effectiveness of alternative substances. One natural substance that has been claimed by some as an effective antidepressant is omega-3 fatty acids, which are found in fish, walnuts, and flaxseed and are available in pill form. Many people take omega-3 fatty acids to reduce high cholesterol as well.

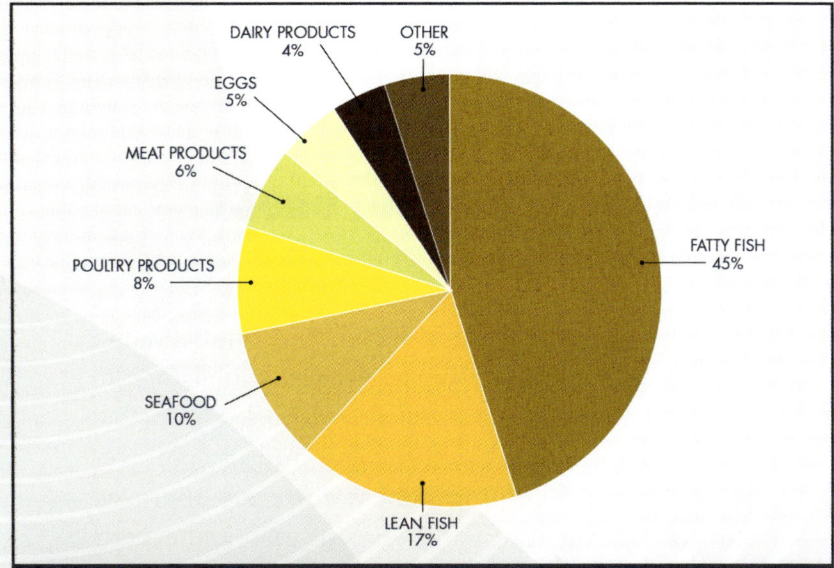

This data from a 2019 study conducted in Poland shows what percentage of the average intake of omega-3 fatty acids comes from certain foods. Even if omega-3 fatty acids do not control BD directly, they are part of a healthy diet, which can help manage the disorder.

People with BD have been found to have lower levels of omega-3 fatty acids that cross the blood-brain barrier—a network of blood vessels that surrounds the brain and filters out unwanted materials—and a number of trials have shown that taking omega-3 fatty acid supplements may help with depression, including the depressive phase of bipolar disorder. However, there is currently no known benefit in the manic phase.

Another compound being tested is uridine. The human liver produces this substance, and it is involved in many body functions, such as the use of energy by cells. There is some evidence that uridine is effective in treating depression in bipolar adults, and in

2011, researchers at the University of Utah tested it in bipolar adolescents. The investigators measured improvements in mood with standardized rating scales. The study found that uridine did decrease depression symptoms and had few side effects in the participants. However, this study included only seven participants, so it suffers from the same limitations as other small-scale studies.

TREATMENT WITHOUT DRUGS

In addition to new types of drug therapy, researchers are evaluating several nondrug treatments. One experimental treatment is deep brain stimulation. In this treatment, doctors implant a nerve stimulator into the patient's upper chest and also place electrodes that receive signals from the stimulator into specific areas of the brain. The procedure is currently approved for the treatment of Parkinson's disease, and experts believe it may also be effective for bipolar patients for whom nothing else works. Brain surgery poses serious risks, such as bleeding, stroke, breathing and heart problems, seizures, movement disorders, and mood and cognitive changes, so doctors emphasize that should it prove effective for BD, deep brain stimulation would only be used in the most severe cases that do not respond to other treatment.

A similar treatment, called vagus nerve stimulation, is less risky but still not widely used for any purpose because of its side effects, which can include hoarseness, coughing, and shortness of breath. It is currently approved to treat unipolar depression that does not respond to other treatments and is being tested in people with BD. With vagus nerve stimulation, doctors insert a small generator attached to wires in the left side of the chest. The wires are connected to the vagus nerve in the neck. The vagus nerve is responsible for relaying signals from the rest of the body to the brain. When the generator in the chest is turned on, electrical pulses are transmitted to areas of the brain associated with depression, and this appears to change the biochemistry in those areas. A newer, less invasive form of this treatment uses electrodes that clip onto the ear. It has also been shown to greatly improve unipolar depression and may also help bipolar depression.

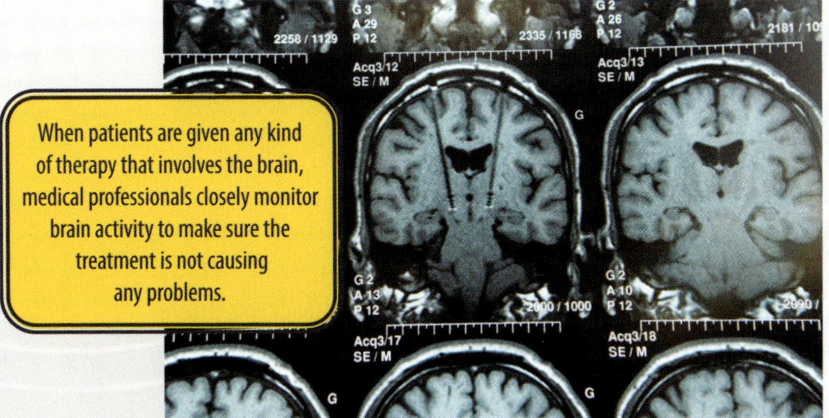

When patients are given any kind of therapy that involves the brain, medical professionals closely monitor brain activity to make sure the treatment is not causing any problems.

Other experimental procedures use magnetic fields rather than electrical currents. One such therapy is magnetic seizure therapy, which is similar to ECT, except it uses a magnetic field to generate a seizure. Like ECT, magnetic seizure therapy is performed when a patient is under general anesthesia. Unlike ECT, which shocks the whole brain, magnetic seizure therapy can be focused on specific areas of the brain. If magnetic seizure therapy proves to be effective, doctors hope it will offer bipolar patients who are not helped by medications a new treatment option.

Another experimental therapy that uses magnetic fields, transcranial magnetic stimulation, does not require the use of anesthesia and can be performed in a doctor's office rather than in a hospital. With transcranial magnetic stimulation, a doctor places an electromagnetic generator on the patient's scalp, and magnetic pulses are sent to parts of the brain that regulate mood. The treatment lasts for 30 to 40 minutes. Experts believe the pulses cause biochemical changes in the brain similar to those that occur during other procedures that use electrical or magnetic stimulation. Transcranial magnetic stimulation seems to be safe and effective for treating unipolar depression, and research suggests that it may also be effective for bipolar depression, although more research is needed to prove these results.

Also effective in treating a kind of unipolar depression is phototherapy, a treatment using light. This treatment often helps people with seasonal affective disorder, which is a type of depression that occurs during the fall and winter months. Doctors have found that the shorter amounts of daylight in winter trigger depression in some individuals.

Light therapy uses a light box or a light visor to deliver bright light to the patient during the time of year when they have symptoms. Sometimes this is administered in a doctor's office, and at other times a patient rents or buys the device to use at home. The patient sits near the light box, and the light must indirectly enter the eyes in order for the treatment to be effective. The individual cannot, however, look directly at the light or it can harm the eyes. A typical treatment session lasts anywhere from 15 minutes to 3 hours, depending on the particular light box and the patient's needs. Side effects are generally mild, when they occur at all, and may include headache, eye strain, and sleep disturbances.

Since light therapy often helps people with seasonal affective disorder, researchers believe it may also be effective for bipolar patients during the depressive phase of their illness. This belief is based on the fact that the internal biological clock that responds to light in the environment is known to play a role in BD. Preliminary studies on several people with bipolar depression showed that light therapy that is done during the middle of the day is often effective in reducing symptoms, but the same treatment in the morning is much less effective and even leads to mixed states in some cases. With seasonal affective disorder, on the other hand, early morning therapy is most effective. Experts are not sure why the effectiveness is different for different types of depression. Although some studies have shown that light therapy can be effective for BD, "researchers say it's important that people with bipolar disorder not try light therapy on their own. First, the results in this study are 'intriguing, but highly preliminary' … And given that light therapy can trigger hypomania … the therapy should be conducted under a doctor's supervision, preferably a psychiatrist."[46]

LOOKING FORWARD

The ultimate goal of the current research efforts—both in the causes and treatment of bipolar disorder—and in the more refined diagnostic criteria is to give people with bipolar disorder a better life as science works toward preventing or more effectively treating the disorder. While those goals are still years away from being reached, the progress of the last few decades in understanding and treating the disease has already made a significant impact on the treatment outcomes for BD patients.

A special light like the one shown here can be helpful for some people with BD.

In addition to the potential treatments already discussed, researchers are looking to genome mapping to explore the possibility of personalized treatment that will target the unique genetic causes of BD in each patient. Others are investigating the patients who respond well to lithium treatment to create a

HEALTHY BODY, HEALTHY BRAIN

While movement alone does not effectively treat bipolar disorder, getting regular physical movement has been proven to enhance the positive effects of other treatment elements. Movement helps people improve their mental health and get better sleep at night. It also helps prevent some of the other health problems, such as heart disease, that often affect people with BD. Some people with BD report that certain types of movement control their symptoms better than others—for example, aerobic exercise such as walking or running tends to improve depression symptoms better than weight training. More research is needed to see how movement affects mania, as some people report that it makes their manic symptoms worse.

The website Everyday Health offered some tips for people who have BD and want to add more movement to their treatment plan:

- ***Pick a form of exercise you enjoy.*** *Don't make it feel like a chore. If you hate running, try something like dancing or swimming. It's more likely you will stick with an exercise you find pleasant.*

- ***Start slowly and work up to a healthy frequency.*** *If you push yourself too hard in the beginning, you might get discouraged and quit. A long-term exercise goal of 30 minutes a day for at least three days a week is optimal [ideal].*

- ***Consult your doctor before beginning*** *… Exercise can interfere with some medications you are taking for your bipolar disorder. You may need to take special precautions when you exercise, such as drinking extra water.*

- ***Find an exercise buddy.*** *The companionship may provide more motivation and good social interaction. Just make sure it's someone who brings calm into your life, not stress.*[1]

1. Regina Boyle Wheeler, "Exercise Can Help Bipolar Disorder," Everyday Health, last updated April 5, 2010. www.everydayhealth.com/mental-health/exercise-can-help-bipolar-disorder.aspx.

genetic test for the disease and to predict the drug's effectiveness in other patients. Meanwhile, advocacy and support groups continue to work to eliminate stigma, educate people, and give people with bipolar disorder hope.

An article from the DBSA sums up the hopeful future for those who live with bipolar disorder and their loved ones:

> *As research continues, we'll understand more and more about the brain and illnesses like depression and bipolar disorder. As time goes on, maybe this new understanding will help us design a better map for those who feel like they are lost in the struggles of life with a mood disorder. And maybe this map will be one of the tools that helps them find their way on the road to recovery.*[47]

NOTES

INTRODUCTION: ON THE RISE

1. Quoted in Irene M. Wielawski, "Diagnosing Mood Disorders in a New Generation," *New York Times*, January 25, 2008. www.nytimes.com/ref/health/healthguide/esn-bipolar-qa.html.
2. Lars Vedel Kessing, Eleni Vradi, and Per Kragh Andersen, "Are Rates of Pediatric Bipolar Disorder Increasing? Results from a Nationwide Register Study," National Center for Biotechnology Information, September 16, 2014. www.ncbi.nlm.nih.gov/pmc/articles/PMC4164856.

CHAPTER ONE: A MISUNDERSTOOD ILLNESS

3. Aretaeus, *The Extant Works of Aretaeus, the Cappadocian*. Edited and translated by Francis Adams. Boston, MA: Boston Milford House, 1972, p. 299.
4. "Bipolar Disorder," National Institute of Mental Health, last updated April 2016. www.nimh.nih.gov/health/topics/bipolar-disorder/index.shtml.
5. "What You Should Know About Mania vs. Hypomania," Healthline, accessed on April 30, 2018. www.healthline.com/health/mania-vs-hypomania#overview.
6. Quoted in David J. Miklowitz, *The Bipolar Disorder Survival Guide: What You and Your Family*

Need to Know. New York, NY: Guilford Press, 2011, p. 20.

7. Aretaeus, *The Extant Works*, pp. 302–303.
8. *Medifocus Guidebook on Bipolar Disorder*. Silver Spring, MD: Medifocus, 2011, pp. 50–51.
9. Chris Iliades, "Is There a Price to Pay for Promiscuity?," Everyday Health, last updated July 15, 2010. www.everydayhealth.com/longevity/can-promiscuity-threaten-longevity.aspx.
10. Quoted in Robert Preidt, "Why Bipolar Disorder Can Take So Long to Diagnose," CBS, July 25, 2016. www.cbsnews.com/news/bipolar-disorder-mental-health-diagnosis.
11. Caroline Miller, "Is It ADHD or Bipolar Disorder?," Child Mind Institute, accessed on May 1, 2018. childmind.org/article/is-it-adhd-or-bipolar-disorder.
12. Andy Behrman, "My Ten-Year Anniversary," *Electroboy*, 2005. www.electroboy.com/article13-tenyearanniversary.shtml.
13. Quoted in "You've Just Been Diagnosed. What Now?," Depression and Bipolar Support Alliance, 2004. www.dbsalliance.org/site/DocServer/FINAL_JustDiagnosed_AYS_AfrAmer.pdf?.docID=2921.

CHAPTER TWO: MULTIPLE CAUSES

14. Aretaeus, *The Extant Works*, p. 302.
15. Christian Nordqvist, "What Should You Know About Bipolar Disorder," Medical News Today, last updated December 7, 2017. www.medicalnewstoday.com/articles/37010.php.

16. Quoted in "Major Ups and Downs," National Institutes of Health, May 2010. newsinhealth.nih.gov/issue/May2010/Feature1.

17. C. A. McClung, "Role for the CLOCK Gene in Bipolar Disorder," Association for Applied Psychophysiology and Biofeedback. www.aapb.org/ar/act-cient/23-McClung_S72.pdf.

18. Derek Beres, "Depression, Schizophrenia, Autism and Other Psychiatric Disorders Show Common Genetic Link," Big Think, February 14, 2018. bigthink.com/21st-century-spirituality/researchers-just-discovered-a-genetic-link-between-alcoholism-autism-bipolar-disorder-depression-and-schizophrenia.

19. Chelsea Lowe and Bruce M. Cohen, *Living with Someone Who's Living with Bipolar Disorder*. San Francisco, CA: Jossey-Bass, 2010, p. 34.

20. Quoted in "Major Ups and Downs," National Institutes of Health.

21. Berit Brogaard, "Bipolar and Testosterone," Livestrong, August 14, 2017. www.livestrong.com/article/494844-bipolar-and-testosterone.

22. Miklowitz, *The Bipolar Disorder Survival Guide*, p. 80.

CHAPTER THREE: OLD AND NEW TREATMENTS

23. Miklowitz, *The Bipolar Disorder Survival Guide*, p. 133.

24. Miklowitz, *The Bipolar Disorder Survival Guide*, p. 7.

25. Denis Campbell, "Lithium Should Be More Widely Used for Bipolar Disorder, Researchers Say," *Guardian*, August 14, 2016. www.theguardian.com/society/2016/aug/14/lithium-should-be-more-widely-used-for-bipolar-disorder-researchers-say.

26. Terri Cheney, "To Lithium or Not to Lithium?," *Psychology Today*, February 8, 2017. www.psychologytoday.com/us/blog/the-bipolar-lens/201702/lithium-or-not-lithium.

27. Cheney, "To Lithium or Not to Lithium?"

28. Gary S. Sachs, et al., "Effectiveness of Adjunctive Antidepressant Treatment for Bipolar Depression," *New England Journal of Medicine*, April 26, 2007. www.nejm.org/doi/full/10.1056/NEJMoa064135#t=articleTop.

29. Quoted in Korina Lopez, "Parents Struggle with Decision to Medicate Bipolar Kids," *USA Today*, December 8, 2012. www.usatoday.com/story/news/nation/2012/12/07/bipolar-kids-parents-medication/1754931.

30. Lopez, "Parents Struggle."

31. Denise Krischke, "Bipolar Disorder and Me," Depression and Bipolar Support Alliance. www.dbsalliance.org/site/News2?page=NewsArticle&id=8237&news_iv_ctrl=1042.

32. "Dual Diagnosis and Recovery," Depression and Bipolar Support Alliance, August 2003. www.dbsalliance.org/pdfs/dualdiag.pdf.

33. "Electroconvulsive Therapy (ECT)," Mayo Clinic, accessed on May 25, 2018. www.mayoclinic.com/health/electroconvulsive-therapy/MY00129.

CHAPTER FOUR: MANAGING BD

34. Krischke, "Bipolar Disorder and Me."
35. Miklowitz, *The Bipolar Disorder Survival Guide*, p. 56.
36. "Anosognosia," Treatment Advocacy Center, accessed on May 25, 2018. www.treatmentadvocacycenter.org/key-issues/anosognosia.
37. Quoted in Hannah Ewens, "Why We Need to Stop Casually Throwing Around Words Like 'Bipolar' or 'OCD,'" Vice, February 15, 2016. www.vice.com/en_us/article/9bgjvz/language-of-catastrophe-why-we-need-to-stop-saying-were-mental.
38. Quoted in Ewens, "Why We Need to Stop."
39. Ewens, "Why We Need to Stop."
40. Quoted in Nancy Tobin, "The Wit and Wisdom of Carrie Fisher," *bp*, February 1, 2010. www.bphope.com/item.aspx?id=630.
41. Quoted in Nancy Tobin, "Next to Normal: Tackling Stigma from the Stage," *bp*, November 1, 2009. www.bphope.com/item.aspx?id=593.
42. Michelle, "A Teen Trying to Live," Depression and Bipolar Support Alliance, March 27, 2006. www.dbsalliance.org/site/News2?page=NewsArticle&id=6068&news_iv_ctrl=1042.
43. Behrman, "My Ten-Year Anniversary."

CHAPTER FIVE: EMERGING RESEARCH

44. Anne Harding, "Ketamine Lifts Mood Quickly in Bipolar Disorder," Reuters Health, August 3, 2010. www.reuters.com/article/2010/08/03/us-ketamine-bipolar-idUSTRE6725J820100803.

45. "Double-Blind Placebo-Controlled Trial of Riluzole in Pediatric Bipolar Disorder," National Institutes of Health Clinical Center, December 24, 2011. www.clinicaltrials.gov/ct2/show/NCT00805493?term=bipolar+disorder+OR+manic+depressive+illness+OR+bipolar+depression+OR+mood+disorders+OR+cyclothymic+disorder+OR+mania+OR+mixed+bipolar+disorder&recr=Open&fund=0&rank=1.

46. Patti Neighmond, "Light Therapy Might Help People with Bipolar Depression," National Public Radio, November 27, 2017. www.npr.org/sections/health-shots/2017/11/27/561574259/light-therapy-might-help-people-with-bipolar-depression.

47. "Treatment Technologies for Mood Disorders," Depression and Bipolar Support Alliance, 2009. www.dbsalliance.org/pdfs/EmrgTechsBro09.FINAL.pdf.

GLOSSARY

acute: Characterized by a sudden and severe flare-up of symptoms.

anosognosia: A symptom of mental illness in which it difficult for the patient to understand that they have a mental illness.

anticonvulsive: A drug usually used to treat epileptic seizures that is also effective in treating bipolar disorder.

chronic: Ongoing and long-lasting.

elation: Great happiness and exhilaration.

electroconvulsive therapy: Medical treatment involving an electric shock to the brain that generates a seizure; the effect is a sort of "rebooting" of the brain.

erratically: In a way that lacks consistency or predictability.

gene: A sequence of DNA that passes hereditary information from parents to their offspring.

general practitioner: A doctor whose practice is not limited to a specialty.

neuron: A nerve cell.

neurotransmitter: A brain chemical that allows neurons to communicate.

psychotherapy: Treatment of mental illness, generally by using talk and behavior modification therapies.

psychotic: Referring to psychosis, a symptom of some mental illnesses that is characterized by an inability to distinguish fantasy from reality.

rapid cycling: A condition where a bipolar patient has four or more episodes during a twelve-month period.

relapse: A recurrence of symptoms.

stigma: A set of negative beliefs an individual or society holds about a particular topic.

synapse: A tiny gap between nerve cells.

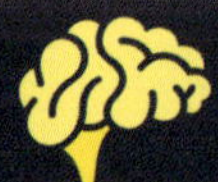

Bipolar Caregivers
bipolarcaregivers.org
This website is aimed at people who are supporting someone with bipolar disorder. It offers tips on how to help the person through different situations, such as manic and depressive episodes. It also includes tips on how the support person can take care of themselves. Many supportive loved ones put their own needs aside to focus on the person they are supporting, but taking breaks to focus on your own well-being is crucial when you are supporting a person with a severe illness.

Depression and Bipolar Support Alliance (DBSA)
55 E. Jackson Boulevard, Suite 490
Chicago, IL 60604
www.dbsalliance.org
Instagram: dbsalliance
YouTube: DBSAlliance
DBSA is a nonprofit organization that seeks to better the lives of people with depression and bipolar disorder through support, education, research, and advocacy. Its website offers information on every aspect of bipolar disorder, including how to help a loved one with the disorder and how to find a local support group.

The Jed Foundation
745 5th Avenue
Suite 500
New York, NY 10151
jedfoundation.org
Instagram: jedfoundation
TikTok: jedfoundation
YouTube: jedfoundation
This nonprofit organization works with schools to prevent suicide and improve mental health for students. The website offers information for people who are seeking help for themselves as well as people who are looking for ways to help a friend.

Juvenile Bipolar Research Foundation (JBRF)
17595 Harvard Avenue
Suite C-616
Irvine, CA 96214
YouTube: juvenilebipolarresearchfou3393
This organization works to understand more about bipolar disorder specifically in children and teens so more effective treatments can be developed.

National Suicide Prevention Hotline
(800) 273-8255
suicidepreventionlifeline.org
People with bipolar disorder are at a high risk for suicide. Anyone who is feeling suicidal can call the hotline or use the live chat option on the organization's website to talk to someone about their problems. Both the phone line and the chat are available 24 hours a day, 7 days a week across the United States.

FOR MORE INFORMATION

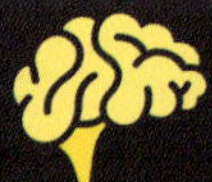

BOOKS

Davis, Rachael. *A Mind Like Mine.* London, UK: Francis Lincoln Children's Books, 2022.

Forney, Ellen. *Rock Steady: Brilliant Advice from My Bipolar Life.* Seattle, WA: Fantagraphic Books, 2018.

Gagne, Tammy. *Living with Bipolar Disorder.* San Diego, CA: BrightPoint Press, 2024.

Taylor, Susan Johnston. *Selena Gomez.* Mankato, MN: Apex Editions, 2025.

Van Dijk, Sheri, and Karma Guindon. *The Bipolar Workbook for Teens: DBT Skills to Help You Control Mood Swings.* Oakland, CA: Instant Help Books, 2010.

Wilson, Steven W. *Teetering on a Tightrope: My Bipolar Journey.* Meadville, PA: Fulton Books, 2022.

WEBSITES

bp Magazine
bphope.com
Published four times per year, *bp* is filled with articles by and about people who share the challenge of living with bipolar disorder. The magazine is an excellent roundup of news, research, and ideas on how to get better care.

iPrevail
www.iprevail.com
Seeking help is important for those with bipolar disorder, but many people have difficulty accessing affordable mental health care. The website iPrevail, which is also available as an app for iPhone and Android, allows people to chat about their problems for free with a trained, non-licensed listener. For $9.99 per month, the user can access licensed therapists. Always ask a parent or guardian before purchasing a subscription.

Mental Health America: Bipolar Disorder
www.mhanational.org/conditions/bipolar-disorder
The Mental Health America website has information about the different types of bipolar disorder as well as a free screening test. The test does not provide a diagnosis, but it can help someone decide whether they should seek help from a psychiatric professional.

The National Alliance on Mental Illness (NAMI)
nami.org
NAMI is the leading grassroots, self-help, and family advocacy organization in the United States dedicated to improving the lives of people with brain disorders. NAMI is active in the research and political arenas and campaigns actively against discrimination and for access to treatment.

TeensHealth: Bipolar Disorder
kidshealth.org/en/teens/bipolar.html
This website provides information on all aspects of bipolar disorder for teens.

INDEX

N

O

P

Q

R

PHOTO CREDITS

Cover, Trzykropy/Shutterstock.com; cover, pp. 1, 3-104 Trisno Wardana/Shutterstock.com; cover, pp. 1, 3, 4, 6, 12, 30, 45, 62, 74, 86, 92, 96, 98, 103, 104 Sentavio/Shutterstock.com; p. 14 fizkes/Shutterstock.com; p. 15 Estrada Anton/Shutterstock.com; p. 17 chayanuphol/Shutterstock.com; p. 20 ranaraya/Shutterstock.com; p. 23 Leszek Czerwonka/Shutterstock.com; p. 25 VH-studio/Shutterstock.com; p. 32 D. Kucharski K. Kucharska/Shutterstock.com; p. 33 New Africa/Shutterstock.com; p. 36 PeopleImages.com - Yuri A/Shutterstock.com; p. 38 Edit 4 Me/Shutterstock.com; p. 40 Pheelings media/Shutterstock.com; p. 43 Bricolage/Shutterstock.com; p. 48 Sonis Photography/Shutterstock.com; pp. 53, 78 luchschenF/Shutterstock.com; p. 56 Daniel M Ernst/Shutterstock.com; p. 59 Frame Stock Footage/Shutterstock.com; p. 64 Monkey Business Images/Shutterstock.com; p. 67 Tinseltown/Shutterstock.com; p. 69 Miljan Zivkovic/Shutterstock.com; p. 71 Chay_Tee/Shutterstock.com; p. 73 EF Stock/Shutterstock.com; pp. 81, 83 Image Point Fr/Shutterstock.com.

ABOUT THE AUTHOR

SIMON PIERCE grew up in Jamestown, NY. He later moved to New York City and completed his education at NYU. Currently, he lives in Brooklyn with his partner and their son. He has written for various health and wellness publications over the past 14 years. He and his family enjoy people-watching in the park, taking road trips to the Adirondacks, and watching basketball games.